EDUCATING CHILDREN WITH PROFOUND HANDICAPS

bimh
Publications

EDUCATING CHILDREN
WITH PROFOUND HANDICAPS

Carol Ouvry

First published 1987

© **1987 Bristish Institute of Mental Handicap**
(Registered Charity No. 264786)

Published and distributed by: **BIMH Publications,**
Foley Industrial Park,
Stourport Road,
Kidderminster,
Worcs. DY11 7QG

ISBN 0 906054 58 3

Typeset and printed by: Birmingham Printers (1982) Ltd.,
Stratford Street North, Birmingham B11 1BY

Contents

CONTENTS

Page

8

Acknowledgements

There are many people to whom I am grateful for help and encouragement in the preparation of this book. I have received help from friends and colleagues in many parts of the country but, above all, I must thank all the members of staff at Paddock School with whom I have worked, whose enthusiasm and expertise supported and inspired my own efforts with children with profound handicaps. In particular I must thank Nora Evans, the Headmistress, for unfailing encouragement in every aspect of development of the Special Needs Department, which provided me with the experience upon which the book is based.

CO

Part 1

Management and integration of children with profound handicaps

---

Introduction

Since the implementation of the 1970 *Education Act* and the provision of education for all children regardless of the degree of mental handicap, the curriculum for children with severe learning difficulties has been widely developed. However, a significant number of children with profound mental handicaps, many of whom have additional physical and sensory impairments, are unable to participate in the activities which form the curriculum for their peers in schools catering for pupils with severe learning difficulties.

The number of pupils with profound and multiple handicaps, both in local education authority schools and independent establishments, is increasing. Medical progress ensures that more babies with serious mental and physical defects will survive to school age; with the result that more children whose handicaps are of a severe degree will require school placements. Since the emphasis is now on community care, many children who would once have been hospitalised because of the severity of their handicaps are remaining with their families. Others, who are already in residential establishments, are now being transferred back home or, if this is not possible, to community hostels from which they attend a local school.

Most schools for children with severe learning difficulties have at least one special class for pupils with profound and multiple learning difficulties. As the numbers increase more special classes are being formed but, in addition, more pupils are being placed in regular classes within the schools. This will undoubtedly result in many teachers, at some time during their career, finding themselves responsible either for a special class or for one or two pupils with profound or multiple learning difficulties in a regular class.

There are, overall, relatively few children with such handicaps. As a result, their existence is largely ignored in initial teacher training, and teachers' expertise has to be gained in the classroom. Many teachers whose classes now accommodate pupils who are profoundly handicapped have previously had no special interest in, or experience of, working with this group. Some are in their probationary year of teaching. Although acting as the leader of a multidisciplinary team, a teacher working with such pupils may often feel professionally isolated from other teachers; and this isolation is exacerbated by the small amount of published material relevant to teaching this group of pupils.

In the past few years interest in the problems encountered in teaching children with profound and multiple handicaps has become more widespread, and educational research is taking place in establishments throughout the country. Much of this work, however, concentrates on developing individual programmes to achieve specific objectives using the behavioural approach, which are intended to be used in one-to-one teaching sessions. Such material is invaluable to the teacher when identifying teaching objectives for individual children, but it does give a very circumscribed view of working with this group of children since, in practice, much time has to be devoted to group work and less highly structured and intensive activities.

There has, until recently, been virtually no published material which offers guidelines on curriculum development and classroom practice appropriate for pupils with profound and multiple handicaps. Two surveys (Ouvry, 1983; Evans and Ware, 1987) reveal an apparently widespread lack of structure and considerable vagueness about curriculum content, with the emphasis still on caring or entertainment rather than educational activities. There is, therefore, an urgent need for written material which will make existing knowledge readily accessible to teachers.

Part 1 of this book attempts to provide relevant information and theory, and to discuss issues which form the background for planning the curriculum for pupils with profound and multiple learning difficulties. It is based on classroom experience and the results of a survey carried out by the author in 12 schools in 1982/3 (Ouvry, 1983). The intention is to provide a basis of knowledge and ideas which will be of value to all teachers who are new to this field of special education.

References

Evans, P., Ware, J. *Special Care Provision: the Education of Children with Profound and Multiple Learning Difficulties.* Windsor: NFER-Nelson, 1987.

Ouvry, C. *Considerations in Planning the Curriculum for the Profoundly Handicapped Child.* (Unpubl. thesis.) London: Univ. London Institute of Education, 1983.

CHAPTER 1

Profound handicap

There are many definitions of mental handicap, which may be expressed in terms of intelligence quotient (IQ), behavioural competence, or need for special services. The World Health Organisation uses four categories based on IQ level: mild, moderate, severe, and profound. It describes impairments of intelligence as including "disturbances of the rate and degree of development of cognitive functions, such as perception, attention, memory, and thinking, and their deterioration as a result of pathological processes". Each category is defined both by IQ level and the ability to acquire varying degrees of personal and social skills with appropriate training (WHO, 1980).

Similar categories were used in this country in the past and were distinguished by the terms moron (IQ 50-75), imbecile (IQ 30-50), and idiot (IQ under 30). However, after the 1959 *Mental Health Act* these emotive labels were replaced by the terms subnormal and severely subnormal, the dividing line being an IQ of 50. The importance of these two categories lay in the fact that "the subnormal" were considered to be educable and were thus the responsibility of the education authorities, whereas "the severely subnormal" were considered to be ineducable and responsibility for them lay with the health authorities. The 1959 *Mental Health Act* defines severe subnormality as "a state of arrested or incomplete development of mind which includes subnormality of intelligence and is of such a nature and degree that the patient is incapable of living an independent life or of guarding himself against serious exploitation, or will be so incapable, when of an age to do it" (Mittler, 1976). This clearly refers not only to the intelligence but also to the competence of the individual to cope with a normal social environment. Other definitions of mental handicap stress the inability of the individual to function effectively and to "meet age and cultural group standards of personal independence and social responsibility" (Winnick, 1979).

In the 1983 *Mental Health Act* the terms subnormal and severely subnormal have been replaced by "mental impairment" and "severe mental impairment". Mental impairment is defined as "a state of arrested or incomplete development of mind which includes significant impairment of intelligence and social functioning and is associated with abnormally aggressive or seriously irresponsible conduct". Severe mental impairment requires that impairment of intelligence and social functioning is of a "severe" rather than "significant" degree. This change of emphasis, from social competence and vulnerability to deviant behaviour, limits the responsibility of health authorities for provision for people who are mentally handicapped. This has, since the time of the 1970 *Education (Handicapped Children) Act,* been increasingly taken on by the education authorities and social services. Since the *Court Report* (1976) this shift of responsibility has been gathering momentum and patients have begun to be transferred from hospital to community based services.

After the 1970 *Education (Handicapped Children) Act,* the two groups defined by the 1959 *Mental Health Act* were referred to, in educational terms, as educationally subnormal (mild) or ESN(M), and educationally subnormal (severe) or ESN(S). Schools and support services were for the first time provided to cater for the needs of children categorised ESN(S). These schools became part of the special education provision which consisted of separate schools or units catering for 11 different categories of handicap. Children were placed in the most appropriate type of school according to their primary handicap.

The 1981 *Education Act* came into force in April, 1983. It was based on the recommendations of the *Warnock Report* (1978) which identified a much larger group of children (20 per cent of the total school age population) who would at some time during their school career have a special educational need of either a temporary or permanent nature. Most of these children were being educated in ordinary schools but about two per cent of them were attending special schools. The 1981 *Act* related special educational need to learning difficulty which it deemed was present:

if a child had significantly greater difficulty in learning than the majority of his peers;

if a child had a disability which prevented him from benefiting from the education generally provided by the local education authority; or,

if a child, under school age, was likely to fall into one of the above groups.

The categories of handicap previously used were replaced by provision for assessment of the child in close consultation with the parents followed, if necessary, by a formal Statement of the child's individual needs in terms of education and a recommendation for placement and support. Special schools which were formerly for ESN(S) pupils were redesignated as schools for children with severe learning difficulties.

Prevalence and aetiology of severe mental handicap

The proportion of children with an IQ of 50 or below, who represent the lowest end of the normal curve of distribution of intelligence, would be expected to be in the order of 0.04 per cent but the prevalence of severe mental handicap is considerably higher at around 0.35 per cent of the population of school age (Weddell, 1975). Many authorities have suggested that the aetiology of mental handicap comprises two distinct subgroups, sociocultural and clinical, which helps to explain the excess of those who are severely handicapped.

Children in the sociocultural group, who represent the lower part of the normal distribution curve of intelligence, seldom have any marked physical or physiological abnormalities. The prevalence of this sub-group corresponds to the proportion of the population which would be expected in a normal distribution.

The excess of children with severe mental handicap make up the clinical, or pathological, sub-group which has its own frequency curve lying at the lowest end of the normal distribution curve (see Fig 1).

In the majority of these children the cause of the handicap is some kind of influence during the development of the foetus or infant. These causes are commonly classified according to the time at which they occur. Prenatal causes include genetic and chromosal abnormalities, infections during pregnancy, and external influences such as intoxication, drug abuse, and irradiation. Green (1985) states that in the Western world it is probable that 75 per cent of severe mental handicap is attributable to prenatal influences. Perinatal causes include birth trauma, asphyxia, infection, and jaundice, any of which may damage the newborn baby and result in cerebral palsy with or without additional mental handicap.

This is borne out by Green (1985) who states: "It is very unusual for birth problems to give rise to mental retardation *per se* in the absence of physical findings". Postnatal causes include severe

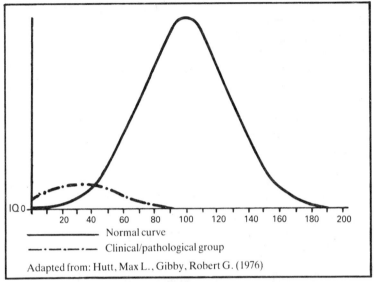

Normal curve

Clinical/pathological group

Adapted from: Hutt, Max L., Gibby, Robert G. (1976)

FIGURE 1. Frequency distribution of intelligence quotient

infections such as meningitis and encephalitis, accidental and non-accidental injuries, and cardiac arrest associated with some other medical condition such as epilepsy.

Cooper, Liepman, Marker, and Schieber (1979) have noted that the frequency of associated handicaps increases with the declining level of intelligence. Research has shown that, in this group, between 80 and 90 per cent of children have handicapping conditions of a physical, sensory, dysmorphic, or biochemical nature in addition to their severe mental handicap (Bernsen, 1981; Yule, 1975; Mittler, 1979).

Definition and effect of profound handicap

It is not surprising in view of the above findings, that there is a significant group of pupils in schools for children with severe learning difficulties whose handicaps are so severe, or who are operating at such an early developmental level, that they require special provision within those schools. The problem of defining such a heterogeneous group has been widely noted (Hogg and Sebba, 1986) and there is consequently a wide variety of names used to refer to the children (Evans and Ware, 1987). In this book they are referred to as children with profound handicaps.

Although in the sphere of education it is now usual to use the term "learning difficulties", the nature and severity of the disabilities of the children with whom this book is concerned is such that their problems go beyond learning difficulties. The children are, in fact, handicapped in virtually all aspects of their lives. Kirman and Bicknell (1975) refer to three groups of children whom they consider to fall into this category:

"those who may arbitrarily be defined as achieving an intelligence quotient of less than 20 if a standard test can be applied to them;

those children with multiple disabilities, in particular non-ambulant children with cerebral palsy or spina bifida;

those children who have very disturbed behaviour, who are overactive or withdrawn or non-communicating, destructive or self-destructive."

It is children in the first two groups, who are functioning at such a low level that assessment of IQ would be meaningless or whose severe additional handicaps compound their mental handicap, and whose experience and personal independence is, as a result, extremely restricted, who are the subject of this book.

Throughout the term "profound handicap" is generally used for both groups. Where it is necessary to distinguish between groups the children will be said to have "profound mental handicaps" and "multiple handicaps" respectively. Although some of the children may show a degree of behaviour disturbance, this is not their primary handicap. It may well be the result of the frustrations and limitations imposed by their other disabilities, or the demands or restrictions imposed by the environment.

Children who would fall into Kirman and Bicknell's third group, whose behaviour is so disruptive or destructive that assessment is virtually impossible, are not necessarily profoundly mentally handicapped. They may be able to function competently in a regular class if the behaviour disturbance is resolved. Such children are not covered in this book because, although they may well need special provision of some kind, their educational and management needs are different from, and often at variance with, those of children who are profoundly handicapped. For this reason, as well as for the safety of more vulnerable children, they need alternative provision.

Relative number of pupils with profound handicaps

Kirman and Bicknell (1975) and Mittler and Preddy (1981) seem to agree that about 25 per cent of pupils in day schools for children with severe learning difficulties are profoundly handicapped, and that the proportion is likely to be higher in hospital schools. An informal survey of 12 schools in London and the home counties (Ouvry, 1983) showed a slightly lower proportion, of 22.7 per cent. The variety of criteria used in different schools, however, made identification of the children rather arbitrary and this could account for the discrepancy of 2.3 per cent.

In a more recent survey of 36 schools Evans and Ware (1987) found that more children were entering "special care units" than were leaving. This was partly attributable to the policy of returning children from distant residential care to local provision, but the main reason was the increasing number of children being admitted to the schools on reaching school age, in relation to the number transferring to other establishments on reaching school leaving age. This suggests that the number of school-age children with profound handicaps is increasing. In some schools they may account for more than one third of the total number of pupils.

Since the 1981 *Education Act* education statistics have not been gathered on the basis of the 11 educational categories. These, in any case, did not distinguish between pupils with severe and profound handicaps in ESN(S) schools. Figure 2 shows the numbers for 1981,

Children attending ESN(S) schools and classes — 1981	
LEA schools — day	24,517
— residential	537
Non-maintained — day	21
— residential	120
Independent	676
Hospital schools	3,341
Normal schools	269
Home tuition	534
Waiting for admission — day 5+	132
— under 5	285
— residential	39
TOTAL:	30,471
TOTAL SCHOOL POPULATION:	8,720,125
Children following a developmental curriculum — January 1985	
In special schools TOTAL:	34,879
TOTAL SCHOOL POPULATION:	7,955,900

FIGURE 2. Number of children with severe learning difficulties

which are the latest available from the Department of Education and Science, based on categories of schools. They show a total of 30,471 children attending or awaiting admission to ESN(S) classes or schools. This confirms the figure of 0.35 per cent of the total schools population. Of these children at least 7,500 are likely to be profoundly or multiply handicapped, and most of them will need what are frequently known as "special care" classes.

Figure 2 also gives the most recent numbers available, for January 1985. These show that, although the total school population has fallen, more pupils are now following a developmental curriculum in special schools despite the process of integration into mainstream schools which is under way in many education authorities. Since these "integrated" pupils are likely to come from the higher ability range, the implication is that, in authorities where integration is well-established, the proportion of pupils with profound and multiple handicaps in schools for children with severe learning difficulties is likely to be even greater than the absolute numbers would suggest.

Criteria for placement in special classes

Most schools for children with severe learning difficulties have one or more special classes where extra support and a modified curriculum is provided for pupils who are profoundly handicapped. The criteria for placement in these classes vary widely between schools, but they are usually based on the children's disabilities, most frequently identified as multiple handicap, lack of mobility, and cognitive level, and their educational needs (Ouvry, 1983; Evans and Ware, 1987).

Fig 3. shows that of the children in the special classes covered by the 12 school survey (Ouvry, 1983) 74.5 per cent had severe physical abnormalities and 31.6 per cent had sensory deficits. 13.9 per cent exhibited a behaviour disorder, although it was not specified whether this was the primary reason for placement in the special class or whether the behaviour occurred because of their other disabilities. 82 per cent of the children were non-verbal.

The degree of disability which determines placement in a special class varies widely both between and within schools. In some schools children with profound handicaps are placed in the regular classes; in other schools pupils who are less disabled are placed in special classes. Placement decisions may be arbitrarily determined because of the lack of any coherent policy, or they may depend

Number of children in class		Severe physical abnormality		Sensory impairment		Behaviour disorder		Non-verbal	
		No.	per cent	No.	per cent	No.	per cent	No.	per cent
1	23	15	66	3	11	1	4	23	100
2	25	13	52	9	36	4	16	24	96
3	11	8	73	5	45	2	18	11	100
4	17	16	95	10	58	1	5	16	94
5	16	11	69	3	18	1	6	15	93
6	23	21	92	2	8	1	4	20	86
7	10	8	80	6	60	1	1	10	100
8	14	8	58	1	7	3	21	10	71
9	9	9	100	1	11	3	33	8	88
10	12	10	84	4	33	1	8	10	83
11	6	2	34	4	66	2	33	0	0
12	11	10	91	3	27	2	18	8	72
Total:	179	131	74.5	51	31.6	22	13.9	155	82

FIGURE 3. Disabilities of children in 12 special classes

upon the facilities available in the schools, or on the willingness or otherwise of individual teachers to accept children with profound handicaps into their classes. Even where fairly consistent criteria are set, there can be considerable differences between schools.

At one extreme every child is placed in a regular class, regardless of the severity of disability, unless or until the situation becomes impossible for either the child or the teacher, at which point the child is moved into a special class. This approach can be defended on the grounds of "integration" but even if extra staffing is provided, and very often it is not, the timetable is unlikely to cater for the special needs of a child who is profoundly handicapped. Nor is it likely to give priority to, or even include, the curriculum areas which are of greatest importance to such a child. This results in a negative approach, in which the child is expected to fit the provision rather than the provision fit the child's needs. Time spent in this way in a regular class is time lost, and it may easily result in a deterioration of behaviour, or a reduced level of functioning or physical development before transfer to a special class is arranged. Ultimately this policy makes the task of the teacher in the special class more difficult.

At the other extreme children whose handicaps are less severe may be placed in a special class in order to develop the abilities and skills necessary for taking part fully in the curriculum followed by their peer group in the regular classes. Offering special class provision to a larger group of children with a wider range of abilities can also be defended on the grounds of integration, future rather than immediate. The hope is that the children, with extra help in the early years, will be able eventually to function effectively in the regular classroom on a permanent or part-time basis. It may also be argued that the presence of a more active group of children in the special class will widen the scope of the activities undertaken, facilitate the integration process, and enrich the class as a whole. This tends to be a more positive approach, in that placement is expected to concentrate upon each child's individual needs, and to facilitate progress rather than provide containment.

In every school the decision has to be made as to which children will go to the special class and, most importantly, why they will be placed there. If their additional handicaps are so severe, and their stage of development so early, that they cannot participate in or benefit from regular classroom activities or interact with their peer group to any significant extent, placement in a special class is likely to be most appropriate. The modified curriculum, timetable, and teaching techniques there should enable the special class pupils to use their abilities and develop their skills to the greatest possible degree. In coming to any decision about placement it may be helpful to bear in mind the distinctions drawn by Harris (1957) between:

"(1) impairment, the basic biological fault in a tissue or organ;

(2) disability, the limitation of function consequent upon impairment; and

(3) handicap, the resulting personal and social disadvantage".

All three aspects will have a bearing upon whether a child is able to participate in and benefit from regular classroom activities, or whether special class placement is needed. Clearly the child's degree of disability and extent of handicap are closely related to the degree of impairment. These relationships, however, are complex and it is not enough to base decisions upon the nature of a child's impairments *per se* since the child's other attributes and the situational context will also be of prime importance.

It is the child's disability which the educational programme will try to alleviate, thereby reducing the degree of handicap. In addition, specialised support services will help class teachers to reduce or prevent further impairment.

It is the degree of handicap and the child's abilities on the one hand, and the relative ability of the special class or regular class to

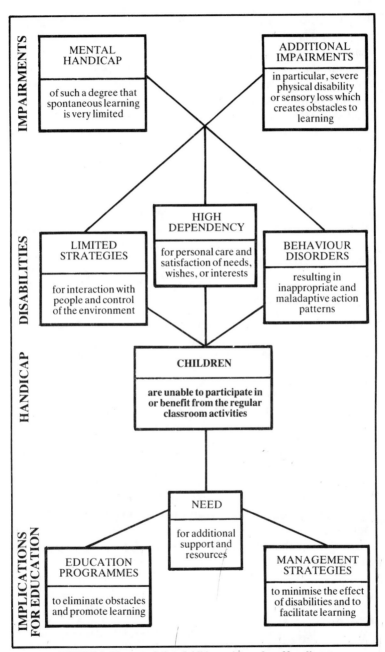

FIGURE 4. Characteristics of children with profound handicaps

offer suitable activities and environment to counteract the impairment and its resultant disability on the other hand, which must be weighed up when considering placement of a child who is profoundly handicapped. No hard and fast rules can apply because each child's profile of disabilities and abilities is unique and each special class offers different opportunities depending upon the number and quality of staff, the extent of outside support, the generosity of provision for specialised equipment, and the space and facilities available.

Children in special classes for pupils with profound handicaps have a very wide range of disabilities, often arising from a combination of mental handicap and additional physical and/or sensory impairments. Every child must be considered individually; but certain generalisations can be made since the net result of the disabilities is commonly a constellation of characteristics (see Figure 4) which includes:

a very high degree of dependence upon others for satisfaction of needs, wishes, and interests;

inappropriate and maladaptive behaviours which are frequently stereotypic and self-stimulatory, or even self-injurious, and which prevent effective interaction with the environment; and

an inability to understand and control surroundings and experiences, with few effective strategies for learning and interacting, either with the surroundings or other people.

Children with profound handicaps are denied many of the everyday experiences which are the initial learning situation for children who are not handicapped. Their disabilities prevent them from using or responding appropriately to the experiences that they do have. Consequently they are unable to participate in or benefit from regular classroom activities. They have special needs, both in terms of education and management, which require additional resources and support.

References

Bernsen, A. H. Handicaps, skills and behaviour of mentally retarded children: an epidemiological research method. *In* Cooper, B. (Ed.). *Assessing the Handicaps and Needs of Mentally Retarded Children.* London: Academic Press Inc., 1981.

Cooper, B., Liepman, M. C., Marker, K. R., Schieber, P. M. Definition of severe mental retardation in school age children: findings of an epidemiological study. *Social Psychol.*, 1979; **14**, 197-205.

Court Report. *Fit for the Future. Report of the Committee on Child Health Services.* (Cmnd. 6684.) London: HMSO, 1976.

Education (Handicapped Children) Act, 1970. London: HMSO, 1970.

Education Act, 1981. London: HMSO, 1981.

Evans, P., Ware, J. *Special Care Provision: the education of children with profound and multiple learning difficulties.* Windsor: NFER-Nelson, 1987.

Green, S. H. An introduction to mental retardation. *Physiotherapy,* 1985; **71**:3, 100-101.

Harris, D. B. (Ed.). *The Concept of Development.* Minneapolis: Univ. Minnesota Press, 1957.

Hogg, J., Sebba, J. *Profound Retardation and Multiple Impairment. Vols. 1 & 2.* London: Croom Helm, 1986.

Hutt, M. L., Gibby, R. G. *The Mentally Retarded Child: development, education and treatment.* Allyn Bacon Inc., Distrib. Hemel Hempstead: Prentice-Hall, 1976.

Kirman, B., Bicknell, J. (Eds.). *Mental Handicap.* London: Churchill Livingstone, 1975.

Mental Health Act, 1959. London: HMSO, 1959.

Mental Health Act, 1983. London: HMSO, 1983.

Mittler, P. (Ed.). *The Psychological Assessment of Mental and Physical Handicaps.* London: Tavistock/Methuen, 1976.

Mittler, P. Educating mentally handicapped children. *In* Craft, M. (Ed.). *Tredgold's Mental Retardation.* London: Ballière Tindall, 1979.

Mittler, P. Preddy, D. Mentally handicapped pupils and school leavers: a survey in North West England. *In* Cooper, B. (Ed.). *Assessing the Handicaps and Needs of Mentally Retarded Children.* London: Academic Press Inc., 1981.

Ouvry, C. *Considerations in Planning the Curriculum for the Profoundly Handicapped Child.* (Unpubl. thesis.) London: Univ. London Institute of Education, 1983.

Warnock Committee, The. *Special Educational Needs: Report of the Committee of Enquiry into the Education of Handicapped Children and Young People. (Warnock Report.)* Cmnd. 7212. London: HMSO, 1978.

Weddell, K. *Orientations in Special Education.* Chichester: John Wiley & Sons, 1975.

Winnick, J. P. *Early movement experiences and development, habilitation, and remediation.* Eastbourne: Holt-Saunders, 1979.

World Health Organisation. *International Classification of Impairments, Disabilities, and Handicaps.* Geneva: WHO, 1980.

Yule, W. Psychological and medical concepts. *In* Weddell, K. *Orientations in Special Education.* Chichester: John Wiley & Sons, 1975.

CHAPTER 2

Educational problems and barriers to learning

Pupils in a special class are likely to be a heterogeneous group, whose members differ in age, medical diagnosis, and level of functioning in all aspects of their development. Even so, the problems encountered in the group as a whole will fall into two main categories: educational problems and management implications. This chapter explores the educational problems and barriers to learning experienced by children who are profoundly handicapped. The management implications will be considered in Chapter 3.

Educational problems include both performance and learning disorders and, although it is very easy to confuse one with the other, it is important to try to distinguish between them. A child's lack of success in an activity or task can be due either to an inability to respond appropriately or to a failure to learn. It is essential to identify where the difficulty lies if an effective teaching programme is to be planned for each child with objectives which are relevant and attainable.

Performance disorders

Performance disorders are common in children who are profoundly handicapped. Most obvious are the difficulties faced by those who have physical disabilities, many of whom encounter considerably restricted voluntary movement and difficulty in controlling what movement they have. Normal active responses are impossible for them. Their degree of intellectual impairment, however, may not be as severe as their physical disability.

The physical disability inevitably creates for these children an added obstruction to intellectual development. It may be necessary to adapt the teaching programme into one which requires responses which will make the maximum possible use of whatever capabilities they do possess. Such a programme will be both realistic and progressive. Additional specialist services, such as physiotherapy or occupational therapy, can play an important part in creating a situation in which learning is facilitated and the achievements of the educational programme are enhanced.

Learning disorders

Learning disorders in children with profound handicaps are similar to those found in the regular classes of schools for children with severe learning difficulties; differing not so much in kind as in degree. The severity of the mental handicap limits the children's access to learning situations and restricts the variety of experience available to them. Van Etten, Arkell, and Van Etten (1980) state: "as the severity of the handicap increases, less incidental learning occurs, and more specific training is required to assure that even the basic life skills are acquired". In addition to the mental and physical handicaps there is a high incidence of sensory impairment, particularly of vision and hearing, in this group of pupils. This limits even further the children's ability to interact with the environment and restricts their everyday experiences.

The information processing model

Learning has been described as a reasonably permanent change in behaviour which grows from past experience. Child (1981) suggests that the change in behaviour may be "the adoption of new, or modification of existing, behaviour patterns, in a way which has some influence on future performance or attitudes". Barriers to learning can occur at any stage of the learning sequence. The information processing model (see Fig 5) is useful in clarifying learning stages and helping to identify the nature of the obstacles which exist for individual children.

INPUT

The first stage in the learning process is the acquisition of information about external or internal conditions. In infants, and in some children with profound handicaps, internal events such as sensations of hunger, thirst, pain, fatigue or cold, relief from such discomforts, and pleasurable sensations, predominate. External events, however, which include any change in the environment of a magnitude that is discernible by the children, are particularly important in the learning process. Awareness of both internal and external events will depend primarily upon the functioning of the sensory receptors and the senses of touch, hearing, and vision provide most of the information upon which learning is based.

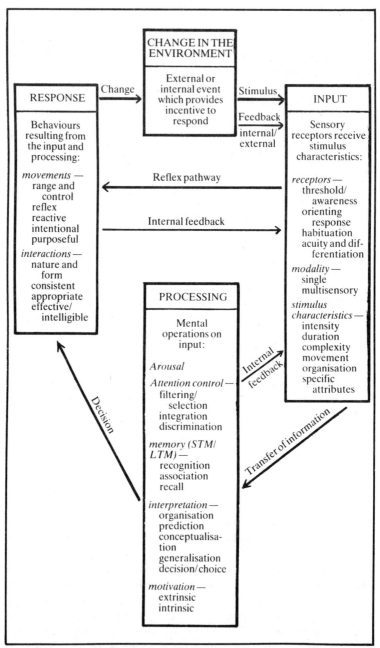

FIGURE 5. Information processing model

It has proved difficult to obtain reliable data on the prevalence of visual, auditory, and dual sensory impairment in children with mental handicaps (Ellis, 1986).

It is true to say, though, that a significant number of children with profound handicaps have severe sensory impairments. Although it is rare to find total loss of any sense, even a moderate impairment of vision or hearing will result in gross distortion of perception. This can result in the children producing inappropriate responses which, in turn, exacerbate the effect of the mental handicap. Mittler (1976) comments that sensory impairments "begin to affect development from the first weeks of life since they deprive the child of visual or auditory experiences at a time when the intact child is already able to make use of them". Where there is a dual impairment of vision and hearing the children's difficulties in gaining useful information from their surroundings are compounded. The distortion, and the consequent confusion which sensory impairment produces, may cause them to avoid using the affected sense. This further reduces the amount and variety of their experience and prevents multisensory integration which could otherwise help to counteract the fragmentation of input of information which they receive.

Encouraging use of the impaired senses

The first task for the teacher may be to promote visual or auditory awareness, and to encourage children to make use of whatever sight or hearing they possess. An orthoptist or audiologist can help to ascertain the severity of the visual or auditory impairments and indicate how much of the resulting behaviour is a direct result of the children's perceptual distortion and how much is a compensatory or avoidance strategy. It is important to establish whether impairment is in the receptors, and is therefore a purely sensory disorder, or whether it is more widespread, resulting in perceptual problems. This may have a bearing on the methods or techniques used to teach each child. It will also allow a realistic expectation of the amount of progress each child is likely to achieve.

Planning the teaching programme

Once some sensory function has been detected a teaching programme must be carefully planned. Appropriate stimuli for individual children must be carefully chosen. They must then be introduced gradually, one at a time, so that the children will not be confused by too many unfamiliar sensations which they are unable to interpret. The general stimulus characteristics of intensity, duration, complexity, and organisation (Zeaman and House, 1979) must be taken into account, as well as the attributes which are specific to particular stimuli in a given context, such as size, shape, colour, novelty, contrast, and their significance to the pupil (Devereux, 1982). The threshold of sensitivity to sensory stimuli will vary between children and between modalities in one child. It will also frequently appear to change from one situation to another. The threshold for each child is the product of the effectiveness of that child's sensory receptors combined with his mental state.

Making the best use of intact senses

As well as increasing children's use of their impaired senses, it is vitally important for the teacher to enhance the acuity of their intact senses. These can be used both to compensate for deficits in the other senses and to extend children's experience.

A deficit in the distance senses of vision and hearing will restrict the area from which children can gain information to their immediate proximity. It will also limit the amount of warning children will receive of an impending event. Teaching programmes should aim to increase each child's tactile sensitivity and body awareness so that they can gain the maximum amount of information possible from their surroundings through tactile exploration and the touch cues they receive from other people.

Sensory integration can be promoted by careful introduction of multisensory stimuli which incorporate properties that are already familiar to pupils. The complexity of experiences offered should be increased gradually until each pupil is able to operate successfully in a multisensory environment.

PROCESSING

In the second, processing stage of learning, information is selected, organised, integrated with the results of previous learning, and a decision is made to respond in a particular manner. Atkinson and Shiffrin (1968), in their research into memory, have distinguished between permanent structures, that is, the physical system and built-in processes which do not vary and are applicable across different tasks and situations, and control processes, that is, strategies which are "selected, constructed, and used at the option of the subject and may vary dramatically from one task to another".

Impairment of the permanent structures creates obstacles to learning through distortion of sensory input over and above that arising from any direct sensory disabilities the children may have, and by reduction of their ability to process the information available to them. Impairment of the control processes will prevent children from establishing the most basic learning skills and thus from using the sensory input to produce appropriate behavioural responses.

In practice it may be difficult to determine whether a child's difficulty stems from impairment of the permanent structures or from inadequate control processes. It is important, however, for teachers to be aware that the education programme can do little to change the permanent structures and must be concerned primarily with encouraging modes of functioning which facilitate learning, thus establishing appropriate learning strategies. It should then provide an environment in which these strategies can be exercised, with controlled input and organised experiences.

Arousal disturbances

A considerable amount of research has been undertaken to identify the physiological functioning underlying the learning and performance disorders of people who are mentally handicapped, but the evidence is inconclusive (Karrer, Nelson, and Galbraith, 1979). Kirman and Bicknell (1975) state that "the most consistent characteristics of brain function in the subnormal are the psychological consequences of disturbances of arousal". Arousal refers to the "tonic state" or relatively stable general level, the phasic spontaneous fluctuations which occur all the time, and reactivity, that is, the tendency to respond to stimuli changes. This influence seems all pervasive at every stage of the learning process, since the threshold of sensory awareness, attention control, memory, and motivation are all affected by the level of arousal at any given time.

Karrer, Nelson, and Galbraith (1979) state that "at our present state of knowledge it appears unproductive to think in terms of 'arousal deficit' in the retarded". Whether or not the origin of the disorder can be conclusively identified the teacher of children with profound handicaps will be familiar with behaviour which ranges from a very low basic level of activity with a reduced sensitivity and delayed reaction to normal stimuli, to behaviour which presents a high level of apparently random or stereotyped activity, a high degree of distractibility, and a tendency for children to over-react to stimuli.

Attention and integration

Attention disorders are commonly found in children who are profoundly handicapped. It has been suggested that the children's inability to sustain attention is the result of a decline of the orienting response to novel or familiar stimuli (depending upon the stage of development) which "increases sensory acuity and facilitates the intake of sensory information" (Karrer, Nelson, and Galbraith, 1979). In addition, the children's inhibitory mechanisms, which filter information and allow selective attention to stimuli, may be inadequate.

It seems that the baseline level of activity could be closely related to problems of attention which result in either a very low level of response and a very fleeting attention span, or a response level which is high and a high level of distractibility. In either case children must be helped to concentrate, to sustain attention, and to become selective so that they perceive the salient attributes of an object or situation. Until this is achieved children will not respond consistently, they will enjoy little meaningful interaction with adults, and will not focus mutual attention with an adult on an object. Under these circumstances teaching cannot occur.

Random stimulation to increase children's awareness and engage their attention is liable to be counter-productive: it may raise their level of arousal, but the children may find it impossible to make sense of, and hence interact with, an environment that is too complicated. In this situation learning will be coincidental and fragmented. Instead, the teacher must choose and present stimuli carefully in order to attract and maintain each child's attention and to encourage an individual response which is both appropriate and consistent.

Even if attention does not present a great problem, the ability of children with profound handicaps to integrate information may be a major obstacle to learning. Birch (1967) has pointed out that "development is characterised not by an increasing proliferation of the senses, but by an increase in the capacity to integrate sensory input". This problem again demands that material is presented in a highly organised and articulated state (Spitz, 1979) so that the salient features and connections are perceived by the children and a body of concepts and meanings is acquired.

Memory

In order to integrate information and make meaningful associations, the selected items must first be stored in the short term memory to remain available while further information is acquired. For learning to take place all the information must be committed to the long term memory to be available in the future.

Short term memory failure will prevent effective integration of information. When presenting new material to the children, the input of information must be maintained long enough to allow the filtering processes to operate so that they can perceive the salient features of the material and make the necessary associations with information they have previously acquired and stored in the long term memory. Failure to produce an appropriate response may be the result of a short term memory deficit or it may be due to the time lag required for processing between input and response. If allowance is not made for this, children may be diverted from their intended response by subsequent input, or the response to the original stimulus will appear inappropriate because further input has intervened.

Impairment of long term memory will affect the availability of previously acquired information because of failure to recognise or recall stored material. This will in turn affect the organisation of experiences and the productive processes of transfer of learning, generalisation, and conceptualisation described by Zeaman and House (1963).

Interpretation, organisation, and generalisation

Interpretation and organisation of information is necessary if it is to be used in the formation of concepts and increasingly complex associations. It permits children to create a model of the world which allows prediction of the consequences of action, expectation in familiar surroundings, and generalisation of skills in a wide variety of situations. Lack of generalisation, that is, the inability to transfer responses learned in one situation to another similar situation, is a common problem. Generalisation is particularly difficult to achieve when behavioural methods have been used in teaching. However, research suggests that this difficulty is not necessarily the result of the children's intellectual limitations and Rostron and Sewell (1984) state that "individuals who received training in a variety of tasks performed better than those who received training on a few tasks". Once a desired response is established, therefore, the teacher must provide a wide variety of situations in which it is appropriate to encourage that response. In this way children will come to appreciate the purpose of their responses in various contexts and will learn to make decisions about the most effective response in a particular situation.

Motivation

In order for children to respond to any stimulus there must be an initial desire to do so and a decision to act on their part. The fact that children do not respond, or do not perform as expected or required, does not necessarily indicate an inability to do so; it may indicate unwillingness, or a lack of motivation.

In seeking a response from a child the teacher is trying to find out whether that child has achieved an objective in the teaching programme. However, Birch (1968) has pointed out that "living organisms are always doing something". If so, the efforts of the teacher are directed towards changing the child's activity rather than instigating activity where there is none. Birch suggests that the tendency to persist in an activity is mediated by habit, arising out of previous reinforcement, and is only changed by forces external to the activity. These forces must be strong enough to elicit an alternative activity and to counteract the persisting tendency. This requires an association to be built up between the instigating force and the desired response by the use of incentives which must be strong enough to supercede the spontaneous activity of the child. This is a development of simple stimulus-response theory in that it takes into account the ongoing activity of the child, and emphasises the fact that the child who, by our criteria, is apparently doing nothing is in fact occupied, even if it is in avoidance of stimulation rather than in seeking or responding to stimulation, or carrying out a purposeful activity. Thus the teacher must be aware of the motivational factors involved in the learning process.

Theories of motivation state that the source of motivation is either intrinsic or extrinsic to the activity. Extrinsic motivation relies upon satisfaction of needs through gaining rewards: tangible rewards such as food; social rewards such as physical contact, praise, or attention; or effectance rewards such as the successful results of action. Intrinsic motivation relies upon the act itself being rewarding rather than, or as well as, it having rewarding results such as increased competence or effectiveness in influencing the environment. Rostron and Sewell (1984) consider that it is doubtful whether the intrinsic motivational aspects of any activity are sufficiently reinforcing to change the ongoing activity of a child who is profoundly handicapped.

In the early stages of a teaching programme tangible or social incentives are more likely to be effective, although problems can arise in finding appropriate rewards for each child. This may well be one of the first objectives of the programme. Ultimately, competence rewards and satisfaction arising from the activity itself may provide some source of motivation for action.

RESPONSE

The third stage of the information processing sequence requires some response from the child as evidence of learning having taken place. Performance difficulties or disorders will be most evident in this stage. Even when children are well-motivated and they have acquired the necessary learning strategies, their actions must be appropriate to the situation and must be carried out in a way that is effective and intelligible to others.

Movements

The most obvious obstacle to achieving the desired result for children who are multiply handicapped is physical disability. This can seriously restrict or distort their movements and can prevent them from carrying out the actions planned. Many children have physical disabilities which, though not severe, will affect the ease and accuracy of their responses. Such disabilities must be taken into account when activities are devised for teaching of skills or assessment of functioning. The amount of concentration required to carry out the physical response, and the time it takes to complete it, detracts from the mental processing which the task involves. This may lead to a memory failure, where pupils forget what they are trying to achieve before the task is completed because of the time and effort involved; or the degree of concentration needed to achieve the desired movement may leave no spare capacity for processing of information in order to carry out the task successfully.

Activities should be chosen for individual pupils in which one aspect lies well within their capability and makes minimal demands upon them, while the main demands of the task lie in an area where learning is intended to take place. It may be necessary for the programme to include activities which are solely concerned with improving physical control and encouraging consistent responses which the children can use later in more complex learning situations. If these approaches are not feasible or successful, perhaps because of the severity of the physical disability or because of lack of motivation, pupils may be helped to overcome or bypass the problems by requiring them to provide alternative responses, or by giving them special equipment which will extend their range of actions without making additional demands upon them. The use of microtechnology is proving to be a valuable teaching aid in this respect, particularly in allowing pupils to communicate choices with a minimum amount of action involved.

Children who are profoundly mentally handicapped but who have no obvious physical or sensory impairment may also exhibit performance disorders, such as inappropriate responses or stereotyped behaviour. They may be operating at a very early stage of development, well below 12 months, and showing behaviour which would be appropriate in its normal developmental sequence but which is both inappropriate and counterproductive in older children. These children appear to function at a developmental level in which circular reactions predominate, having failed to acquire learning skills or strategies to enable them to progress through later developmental stages.

Such children may have an extremely restricted repertoire of actions; lack of basic learning skills and strategies perpetuates the situation. If they do show awareness of objects in the environment, their response may be too fleeting or too stereotyped to allow them to explore their properties. Such exploration could lead to expansion and integration of their experience. Alternatively, the children may show so little interest in the world around them that their only activity is self-stimulation through repetitive behaviour patterns. These behaviours may be pleasurable to the children, but they can also be destructive or self-mutilating. Whatever form they take, such activities effectively exclude any goal directed actions.

Interactions

The sequence of processing information is completed only when children receive feedback from their actions. Bruner (1973) has described three aspects of action which give rise to feedback: *intention,* which is "sometimes called feedforward for it occurs prior to overt action"; *internal feedback,* that is, perceptions arising directly from the action in the form of proprioceptive, visual, auditory, or tactile sensations which inform the children of their actions; and *external feedback,* which arises from the change in the surroundings resulting from the children's actions which will indicate to them whether their actions are effective and conform to their intention. Any sensory impairment will diminish or distort both internal and external feedback and increase any difficulty the children have in making corrections and evaluating the effect of their responses.

Although feedback is generally recognised as being essential to maintain action, this part of the processing sequence is easily overlooked. Children need to know whether their response has been a success or a failure. Initially the signals of success which the teacher uses with the children may be the same as the incentives used to motivate the action in the first place, namely, external rewards such as preferred food, drink, praise, physical contact or attention. Expectation of reward motivates the action, and receiving the reward confirms its effectiveness. As the children's understanding of their surroundings increases, rewards will need to become less tangible, based more upon the satisfactions inherent in gaining competence and effectiveness in different situations and in exerting some degree of control.

Children who are profoundly handicapped may have considerable difficulty at all stages of interaction with the environment: sensory impairments will distort and diminish the input; intellectual impairment will reduce the ability to make meaning out of the input; and physical impairment will reduce their ability to act in an effective way. Both internal and external feedback may be disrupted by the children's impairments. This creates enormous obstructions to their ability to understand and exercise control over their environment and experiences.

Management considerations are therefore twofold: those which relate to the safety and personal care of each child; and those which relate to each child's own functioning. Careful management of the children and the environment is necessary if all pupils are to be enabled to use their abilities to the greatest possible extent, and so attain the greatest possible degree of independence.

References

Atkinson, R., Shiffrin, R. M. Human Memory: a proposed system and its control processes. *In* Spence, K., Spence, J. T. (Eds.). *The Psychology of Learning and Motivation — Vol. 2.* London: Academic Press, 1968.

Birch, D. Shift in activity and the concept of persisting tendency. *In* Spence, K., Spence, J. T. (Eds.). *The Psychology of Learning and Motivation — Vol. 2.* London: Academic Press, 1968.

Birch, H. D., Lefford, A. Visual differentiation, intersensory integration and voluntary motor control. *Monog. of the Society for Research in Child Development,* 1967; **32**:2, 1-87.

Bruner, J. S. Organisation of early skilled action. *Child Devel.,* 1973; **44**, 1-11.

Child, D. *Psychology and the Teacher.* Eastbourne: Holt-Saunders, 1981.

Devereux, K. *Understanding Learning Difficulties.* Milton Keynes: Open Univ. Press, 1982.

Ellis, D. (Ed.). *Sensory Impairments in Mentally Handicapped People.* London: Croom Helm, 1986.

Karrer, R., Nelson, M., Galbraith, G. C. Psychophysiological research with the mentally retarded. *In* Ellis, N. R. (Ed.). *Handbook of Mental Deficiency: psychological theory and research.* New York: Lawrence Erlbaum Associates, 1979.

Kirman, B., Bicknell, J. (Eds.). *Mental Handicap.* London: Churchill Livingstone, 1975.

Mittler, P. J. (Ed.). *The Psychological Assessment of Mental and Physical Handicap.* London: Tavistock/Methuen, 1976.

Rostron, A., Sewell, D. *Microtechnology in Special Education.* London: Croom Helm, 1984.

Spitz, H. H. Beyond field theory in the study of mental deficiency. *In* Ellis, N. R. (Ed.). *Handbook of Mental Deficiency: psychological theory and research.* New York: Lawrence Erlbaum Associates, 1979.

Van Etten, G., Arkell, G., Van Etten, C. *The Severely and Profoundly Handicapped.* C. V. Mosby Co., Distrib. London: YB Medical Publ., 1980.

Zeaman, D., House, B. J. A review of attention theory. *In* Ellis, N. R. (Ed.). *Handbook of Mental Deficiency: psychological theory and research.* New York: Lawrence Erlbaum Associates, 1979.

Zeaman, D., House, B. J. The role of attention in retardate discrimination learning. *In* Ellis, N. R. (Ed.). *Handbook of Mental Deficiency.* London: McGraw-Hill, 1963.

CHAPTER 3

Management implications

Ouvry's (1983) survey showed that almost 75 per cent of pupils being educated in special classes had severe physical abnormalities whilst children with significant sensory impairments made up almost 32 per cent of the total. It is evident from these figures that many of the children will be dependent on others for personal care, including hygiene, eating and drinking, and dressing. In addition, many will require physical support at all times, whether moving about or remaining in one position, necessitating the provision of specialist furniture and equipment to ensure their safety and comfort. Other special educational aids will be required to facilitate their learning.

Children with severe physical abnormalities can place considerable physical demands upon the staff who care for them. If a wide range of educational and therapeutic activities is carried out the work will be very strenuous and may involve occupational hazards such as muscle strain, back injuries, and minor accidents, all of which are risks when moving heavy pupils around in an environment which contains large and cumbersome equipment. An adequate number of staff to cope with the number of pupils is essential, both to enable a comprehensive curriculum to be offered to the children and to protect as far as possible the health and well-being of the staff.

The adult:child ratio varies between schools, depending partly on the generosity of local education authorities in terms of staffing, and partly on the attitude taken in individual schools towards their special classes.

The National Development Group (1977) recommends a staff:pupil ratio of 1:3. Bond (1985) suggests that a ratio of 1:2.5, excluding occasional additional staff (such as members of the medical support services and specialist teachers), is desirable "to enable staff to work preventatively and constructively and to be able to cope with crises, or carry out individual training and programming whilst having adequate cover for other trainees".

Such ratios should be provided as a minimum and for certain activities, such as movement, swimming, outings, and mealtimes, a higher staffing level is advisable.

Personal care and independence

Enabling children to achieve the greatest degree of independence compatible with the limitations imposed by their disabilities is one of the most important aims of education. For those who are most severely disabled this involves allowing time for the use of specific techniques and procedures and providing specialised equipment to ensure safety, comfort, and education, as well as planning individual programmes which promote valuable self-help skills.

TOILETING

In the area of personal hygiene, the most obvious problem is incontinence, and toilet training programmes form an important part of the overall independence programme. Many children will be doubly incontinent, and it is most unlikely that any will be totally independent in using the toilet reliably. Special procedures must be followed for reasons of hygiene and special facilities such as changing couches, supportive bars, and special seating are necessary so that achieving continence does not depend upon the ability to sit unsupported. Other essentials include spare clothing, pads, cleaning materials, and washing and disposal facilities for soiled clothes and pads, all of which take large amounts of space.

Very careful organisation of time, space, and staffing is necessary on the part of the teacher to keep the problem in perspective and to prevent it from assuming enormous proportions and dominating all other classroom activities. Care must be taken to ensure that training programmes are realistic. Children must not be left for long periods without attention; but nor must they spend too much time in over-frequent toilet routines. The nature and degree of intervention will depend upon each child's pattern of toilet needs and the stage of control reached. Since most children with profound handicaps will have no functional speech, a means of communication must be developed for those who have achieved some control but need help because of their physical disabilities. These points are discussed later in the relevant sections of the curriculum.

WASHING AND DENTAL CARE

Washing and dental care also can present difficulties since many children do not easily tolerate these aspects of care and may even resist in any way that is possible for them. Washing face and hands and cleaning teeth is part of the day-to-day routine of the special classroom and forms part of the educational programme of many of the pupils, whether the aim is to increase tolerance of these activities or to establish some self-help skills. Special procedures may be necessary, such as desensitisation of the mouth or face, requiring the advice of a speech therapist or physiotherapist. Teaching can include bathing and hairwashing if these present problems at home and parents or carers feel that a programme carried out in school may help. Again, this may require special equipment, such as bath inserts, bath aids, or shower seats, and the advice of an occupational therapist will be invaluable.

These activities, which contribute to the children's appearance, are vital, both in terms of personal dignity and acceptability to others. Achievement of self-awareness and a degree of participation in these aspects of care can enhance children's self-esteem and, at the same time, ease the burden of care for others.

EATING AND DRINKING

Eating and drinking can vary from total dependence to complete independence, although it is unlikely that children in a special class will be able to use a knife and fork to cut up and eat all kinds of food. Pupils who are totally or partially dependent may need special seating arrangements, crockery or cutlery and, occasionally, special diets. Problems such as tongue thrust, bite reflex, and choking are common, and for some children mealtimes are a potential source of distress and even danger. To overcome this liquidised foods and drinks are sometimes given using a feeding bottle, but this only exacerbates problems by preventing the development of normal control of food and liquid within the mouth. In teaching programmes the consistency of the food must be carefully controlled so that children are encouraged to use the mouth and tongue correctly.

Effective programmes require adequate numbers of staff, who understand the childrens' problems. These staff must be conversant with appropriate techniques, and must know which particular aids are needed by each child. Mealtimes can then be calm and unrushed, and can allow children the maximum opportunity to overcome difficulties and establish good eating and drinking patterns. Careful organisation and appropriate pairing of adults and pupils is essential.

DRESSING

Dressing can be another considerable source of difficulty. Some children may be able to pull some garments on or off, but most will only be capable of minimal cooperation and some will have difficulty in even tolerating the process. Children's physical disabilities, and the deformities which are sometimes associated with them, can make dressing particularly difficult and uncomfortable; special clothes and techniques may be needed to make it easier. For children who have already achieved some degree of continence, it is very important that they acquire adequate dressing skills to help them to become increasingly independent. Even those who can make no active contribution towards dressing themselves can increase their body awareness, tolerance, and cooperation through dressing activities, and so enhance their self-esteem. Those who can make a choice may be able to achieve a degree of self-expression by selecting their own clothes.

MOBILITY

No-one can be fully independent without mobility. The survey carried out by Evans and Ware (1986) showed that lack of mobility is one of the most frequently cited criteria for special class placement. Most pupils in special classes will not only be non-ambulant but will not be independently mobile in any way. A few may be able to move about with adult assistance; a small number may be capable of walking independently but will probably need close supervision to reach their destination.

Movement of the children within and outside the classroom, is therefore a major undertaking when the majority must be pushed, carried, supported, or guided. A sufficient number of strong adults is necessary, as well as equipment in the form of mobility chairs and walking aids of all kinds. Above all, time is needed to complete the operation. Whereas in regular classrooms a change of activity requiring regrouping can be quickly organised, in special classes extra time must be allowed between activities to complete the changeover, thus reducing the time available for lessons.

In addition, the curriculum must provide time for mobility training, walking practice, and weight bearing, all of which involve specialist equipment in the form of standing frames, gaiters, and walking aids of all kinds. The cooperation and participation of children in moving around is vitally important. If they can walk or at least take their own weight, particularly as they grow older and heavier, the burden of care on the staff is eased and this is likely to enable them to offer a greater variety of experiences.

Positioning furniture and equipment

Many children with profound handicaps will be unable to sit unsupported. They will require special seating, both for safety and comfort and for gaining a feeling of security which will allow them to concentrate on the activity in progress rather than on maintaining a safe posture. It is not desirable, either from a therapeutic or educational point of view, for them to remain in one chair and one physical environment all day.

Positioning is a major consideration in all situations. A frequent change of position is vital for physical well being and comfort.

Many children will need different chairs for mobility and working. Wheelchairs are often unsuitable for use when children are working because they do not provide enough support, or because they make the task more difficult for them through the height or angle of the seat. Wheelchairs are often incompatible with the usual school tables, and although they may be fitted with trays these are unsuitable for many activities and can be very restrictive, forming a physical barrier between the children and their surroundings. They also accentuate the difference between children with physical disabilities and their able-bodied peers and can make them appear even more handicapped. A range of tables and chairs of varying heights and sizes, and with special features such as cut-outs to fit round the children and provide support, are necessary to ensure that every child is correctly seated and materials and activities can be presented at the best level and distance for each one.

Some children are unable to tolerate a sitting position. They will need special equipment, like mats, wedges, beanbags, side lyers, prone boards, rockers, and hammocks, so that they can carry out activities whilst reclining on their back, side, or front. This means that they will require considerably more space than children who can sit on an ordinary chair, or unsupported on the floor.

The special classroom, therefore, must be larger than usual to accommodate children's equipment and allow space for working, storage, and moving about safely. Apart from the special furniture and educational equipment already mentioned, there is a large range of therapeutic equipment available. A physiotherapist or occupational therapist will be able to advise on its use with individual children. Such equipment, however, is often large and cumbersome. It can present safety hazards and require considerable space, both in use and storage. The classroom should be organised in a way that minimises the hazards and allows for ease of movement between different work areas. The arrangement must facilitate physical management and hygiene procedures and so permit the greatest possible proportion of time to be spent in educational activities.

To recap, then, adequate facilities and support must be available in the special class to minimise the management problems and allow time for educational activities. There must be a high staff ratio, with additional input from paramedical and specialist staff, extra space, a modified curriculum, and a flexible timetable if each pupil's personal and educational needs are to be met.

Learning materials

As well as special furniture the special classroom needs specialist learning materials. Several firms* now supply materials which, though resembling standard equipment, vary in size or intensity of attributes to make them suitable for use by children with physical or sensory handicaps, the rewards offered and the actions demanded to gain the rewards being more appropriate to the developmental level of this group. Although the range is growing, teacher-made equipment is still likely to be necessary, since the cost of these specially produced materials is often likely to be outside the budget of a single class. Some ideas for making these are included in some of the books listed on pages 44 and 206.

Electronic equipment, which can be operated with a minimal amount of movement, can be extremely valuable. This can range from a simple, battery operated toy which costs a few pounds, to computer controlled toys or equipment which can cost several

*see list of suppliers of specialist learning materials on page 45.

hundred pounds. Many schools have acquired computers which can increase the range and variety of experience available to their pupils with profound handicaps, but these may necessitate additional control devices carefully matched to each pupil's physical and mental abilities. A selection of suitable switches and software inevitably involves a further financial outlay.

Time

The other major requirement of the special class is time. Considerably more time must be allowed for attending to children's personal needs, moving them into teaching groups, positioning them in appropriate or therapeutic ways, and correctly presenting activities so that they can exercise their abilities most easily. The timetable must schedule activities such as independence, in the form of self-help skills or making choices, and mobility, which in regular classes requires little time or takes a different form. Time must be allotted in individual programmes for developing children's physical responses or improving learning skills which are taken for granted in other classes.

The special class curriculum will be determined by the need to compensate for the restricted experiences resulting from the children's handicaps, and to overcome the children's learning difficulties by providing them with activities which will build on, extend, and integrate their abilities and experiences. The aim is to enable them to progress towards the ultimate goals of their educational programmes.

The special class in a school for children with severe learning difficulties can offer more specialised individual programmes because it usually has a higher staff:child ratio, specialised equipment, more space, and a timetable which is flexible and gives priority to the curriculum areas and activities appropriate for children with profound handicaps. Even so, the very wide range of disabilities which are to be found in a special class makes it very difficult, even in the most efficiently organised and flexible timetable, to cater for all the needs of all the children.

It must be remembered that other classes in the school will be able to offer some learning situations which cannot be offered within the special class. The opportunities which exist within the school as a whole must not be neglected. They should, instead, be used to expand and supplement the specialised provision of the special class.

To conclude

Promoting the greatest degree of independence possible in the pupils, and achieving their cooperation and participation in the everyday tasks that must be carried out by their carers, are vitally important areas of the special class curriculum. Their achievement eases the burden of management and care — even more important at home than in school — and may eventually be the decisive factor in the opportunities that can be offered to the school leaver. To succeed in this demands specialist equipment, time, and expertise on the part of the teachers and an organisational structure which ensures the most effective use of all appropriate resources.

References
Bond, D. E. Where next? What next? *Sense*, 1985; **31**:1, 11-13.
Evans, P., Ware, J. *Special Care Provision: the education of children with profound and multiple learning difficulties.* Windsor: NFER/Nelson, 1987.
Ouvry, C. *Considerations in Planning the Curriculum for the Profoundly Handicapped Child.* (Unpubl. thesis.) London: Univ. London Institute of Education, 1983.
National Development Group. *Pamphlet series. No.1 — Mentally Handicapped Children: A plan for action.* London: HMSO, 1977.

Further reading
Anderson, C. A. *Feeding: a guide to assessment and intervention with handicapped children.* Glasgow: Jordanhill College of Education, 1983.
Caston, D. *Easy-to-make Toys for your Handicapped Child.* London: Souvenir Press, 1983.
Finnie, N. *Handling the Young Cerebral Palsied Child at Home.* London: Heinemann, 1974.
Law, I. H. Suckling, M. H. *Handling when children are profoundly handicapped.* Glasgow: Jordanhill College of Education, 1983.
Lear, R. *Play helps: toys and activities for handicapped children.* London: Heinemann, 1977.
Mitchell, S., Ouvry, C. *Make it Simple: Easy-to-make Toys for Profoundly Handicapped Children.* 1985 (Unpubl). Available from the authors — see page 206.
Ouvry, C. Using Electronic Equipment in the Curriculum for Profoundly/Multiply Handicapped Children. *Bulletin of the ILEA Consortium.* London: Jack Tizard School, 1986.
Riddick, B. *Toys and Play for the Handicapped Child.* London: Croom Helm, 1982.
Walsall Working Party on Curriculum Development for the Multiply Handicapped ESN(S) Child. *Teaching the Multiply Handicapped.* Walsall: Walsall Education Department, undated (OOP).
Warner, J. *Helping the Handicapped Child with Early Feeding.* Winslow: Winslow Press, 1981.
York-Moore, R., Stewart, P. *Management of the Physically Handicapped Child. 1 — Guidelines to Handling. 2 — Guidelines to Lifting, Carrying and Seating.* Kidderminster: BIMH Publications, 1982 (OOP).

Suppliers of specialist learning materials

E. J. Arnold and Son Ltd. — Parkside Lane, Dewsbury Road, Leeds LS11 5TD (0532) 772112.

Bradford Activity Toys — 103 Dockfield Road, Shipley, West Yorkshire BD17 7AR (0274) 596030.

Deron Ltd. — Unit 8, Foundry Lane, Byker, Newcastle-upon-Tyne NE6 1LH (091-276) 0660.

Edu-play — 10 Vestry Street, Leicester LE1 1WQ (0533) 25827.

Hestair Hope Ltd. — St. Philip's Drive, Royton, Oldham OL2 6AG (061-652) 1411.

Huntercraft — Ramsam Stable, Priestlands Lane, Sherborne, Dorset DT9 4PD (0935) 812288.

LDA Ltd. — Duke Street, Wisbech, Cambs. PE13 2AE (0945) 63441.

NACRO Handicap Aids Workshop: Unit 9 Sandy Way, Amington Industrial Estate, Tamworth, Staffs. B77 4DS (0827) 51587.

Nottingham Handcraft Ltd. — 17 Ludlow Hill Road, Melton Road, West Bridgford, Nottingham NG2 6HD (0602) 234251.

ROMPA - Pressure Sealed Plastics Ltd. — PO Box 5, Wheatbridge Road, Chesterfield, Derbyshire, S40 2AE (0246) 211777.

Toys for the Handicapped — 76 Barracks Road, Sandy Lane Industrial Estate, Stourport-on-Severn, Worcs. DY13 9QB (02993) 78820.

CHAPTER 4

Integration of children with profound handicaps

Prior to the *Education (Handicapped Children) Act* of 1970 all children with severe mental handicaps were officially considered to be ineducable. They were the responsibility of health authorities which provided training centres and hospital accommodation for them. The 1970 *Act,* however, drew these children into the orbit of education. There has since been a growing emphasis on "integration" as the basis for health, welfare, and education provision, supported by a series of reports and Acts of Parliament in which the statutory obligations of local health, social services, and education authorities are laid down.

Care in the community

The Court Report (1976) emphasised the value of community health care and made recommendations for a two-tier system of child health services based on comprehensive primary care linked with consultant and hospital care. The development of community support services was intended to reduce the number of children who were in institutional care.

The 1983 *Mental Health Act* is primarily concerned with patients who are mentally impaired or severely mentally impaired, whose behaviour is likely to result in them being detained in hospital for treatment for the safety of themselves or others or received into guardianship. People with mental handicaps who do not exhibit such behaviour have been removed from the jurisdiction of mental health law. As a result, the most severe form of segregation — children living in institutions which are often geographically isolated, difficult to reach by public transport, and a considerable distance from their family home — has decreased considerably. Few children with mental handicaps are now admitted to such institutions and a concerted effort is being made to return those who are already resident to their own homes or to other community provision as the local support services develop.

As provision for community care increases, a growing number of children with profound or multiple handicaps will attend local schools for pupils with severe learning difficulties. Many already do so. It is likely, therefore, that in future a greater proportion of children in each school will have special educational and management needs.

Educational integration

A major impetus towards integration within the education service has been the recommendations made in the Report of the Warnock Committee (1978) which regarded handicap, and the resulting educational needs, as a continuum from normal to the most severe. As a result, the Department of Education and Science (1980) stated that not only should special educational arrangements be extended to a much wider range of children, but also that a "child with special educational needs shall be educated with children without such needs, provided that the arrangements are capable of meeting his needs, are compatible with the efficient education of the children with whom he is to be educated and with the efficient use of public resources and take proper account of the wishes of his parents".

The Warnock Committee (1978) suggested three broad areas of educational need: firstly, the need for a special means of access to the curriculum, in which special equipment and facilities are necessary to enable children to participate in activities which their disabilities would otherwise preclude; secondly, the need for a modified curriculum, to cater for intellectual or educational retardation; and, thirdly, the need for a special social structure and emotional climate to enable children with psychiatric or behavioural disturbance to benefit from education.

The Committee also described three different types of integration: locational, in which children with special educational needs are geographically integrated, sharing premises and facilities with other children; social, in which interaction is facilitated by the children coming together at certain times of the day, such as play time, meal times, and for extracurricular activities; and functional, in which children are educated together either on a full-time or part-time basis. The Committee did not suggest that integration is necessarily appropriate for every child but that there should be a continuum of provision ranging from full integration in mainstream schools through to that which can be offered in institutions, and it outlined the support which might be necessary for both children and teachers in achieving the appropriate level of integration.

The 1981 *Education Act,* which was based upon the recommendations of the Warnock Committee, abolished the classification of schools according to the category of handicap of their pupils. It also provides for every child with special educational needs to have the protection of a Statement which identifies those needs and recommends the most appropriate form of education, including the facilities, equipment, staff, and curriculum, to meet them. The Statement also indicates the place where the child's special needs can be met, and suggests any additional services, such as speech therapy or physiotherapy, that may be required.

The *Fish Report* (1985) suggested that integration should be regarded as a process which, to be successful, must involve children in planned interaction with their contemporaries and allow them freedom to associate with different groups. Placement is an essential pre-requisite for carrying through this process, but placement on its own cannot be equated with integration.

Although the Warnock Committee, the 1981 *Education Act,* and the *Fish Report* all refer to children with special educational needs — whether these are temporary or permanent and whatever the degree of severity — being integrated with children who do not need special provision, the concepts are also valid and useful when considering the integration of pupils with profound handicaps with pupils in the regular classes of schools for children with severe learning difficulties. Children with profound handicaps are likely to have needs which correspond to the three broad areas identified by the Warnock Committee: a "special means of access to the curriculum" in the form of equipment, space, time, and teaching techniques; a "modified curriculum" designed to encourage acquisition of relevant skills and knowledge at an appropriate level in an extended time schedule; and a "special social structure and emotional climate" in order to overcome barriers to learning which their behaviour creates.

Although the criteria for placement in a special class varies from school to school the number of children with profound or multiple handicaps in any school for children with severe learning difficulties is likely to be at least 25 per cent of the total number of children on roll. Ouvry (1983) found that 75 per cent of children identified by such schools as profoundly handicapped were placed in special classes. Most schools reported that individual children from the special classes joined other groups on a regular basis for various classroom activities. In a few schools small groups of children from both regular and special classes were formed for specialised sessions such as conductive education (Cotton, 1980) and music. Such arrangements were the result of initiatives taken by individual members of the teaching or support staff, and were not the result of a whole school integration policy.

Despite examples of this kind many special class children can be expected to spend their entire school life in one or two classes and, if they attend a school in which the special class is isolated and there is little integration with the rest of the school, in only one part of the school, in contact with a small number of adults. Such segregation within school must exacerbate the limitations inherent in the condition of profound handicap.

Some schools try to counteract segregation by placing children with profound handicaps in the regular classes, but this can also have disadvantages. The expertise that could be used to provide them with a modified curriculum and effective access to it, may not reach them if they are scattered throughout the school unless there is very careful planning and adequate support.

The special class offers a physical environment which is suitable for meeting the high level of personal dependence of children with profound handicaps and the management and educational problems which result from their disabilities. Its resources include a curriculum designed to cater for the additional learning problems associated with multiple disability or profound mental handicap, and a high level of staffing and specialist support services with which to implement that curriculum.

The criteria for placement in a special class are usually that the children have needs or disabilities which prevent them from participating in or benefiting from the activities carried out in regular classes. Why, then, is integration considered beneficial when the special class offers such a favourable learning environment?

Benefits for children with profound handicaps

All too often children with profound handicaps endure a double segregation. Not only do they attend special schools, but they are isolated within those schools in a special class. However appropriate the special class curriculum, and however well-resourced special classes may be, the children's range of experiences will inevitably be restricted; especially if a school has only one special class, or two or more special classes which operate entirely separately.

In setting out the basic principles of integration the *Fish Report* (1985) stresses the importance of children having equal access to an acceptable range of opportunities, being enabled to make choices and determine lifestyles, and to become responsible participants in the community. These principles, in their widest sense, may seem unrealistic for children with profound handicaps. Nevertheless it is essential to provide them with the least restrictive environment possible and opportunities for wider experiences in which they can practise skills learned in the classroom and make choices in a variety of situations.

LOCATIONAL

It is vital to introduce some variation into the physical environment of pupils with profound handicaps and to involve the children in a variety of experiences which will allow them to form associations between places and specific activities: the taste, smell, and sound of food preparation and domestic activities in the home skills area; the visual impact, smell, and texture of paint and creative materials in the craft room; the physical experience of swimming in the pool or movement sessions in the hall. All these will help children to acquire a greater understanding of their surroundings.

Locational integration, even within one school building, can be difficult. Special classes are often sited away from the centre of the school, with passages, doors, steps, and other obstructions between the special class and the rest of the school. The logistical problems of moving non-ambulant children means that use of the school facilities often demands a high degree of determination on the part of the staff.

The extent to which integration takes place depends partly upon ease of access to various parts of the school and partly upon the school's integration policy. For integration to occur that policy must stipulate that the children based in the special class must have equal opportunities with the other pupils to use available facilities, whether on or off the school site, such as the hall, specialist teaching areas and equipment, community provision such as playgrounds and swimming pools, and places for educational visits.

SOCIAL

Social integration extends the benefits gained through locational integration by arranging for children from the special class to use school facilities at the same time as children from regular classes. Such occasions are likely to include out-of-class activities which involve the whole school, like assembly, singing sessions, play times, meal times, and special events, such as sports day or seasonal festivities. They may also include occasions which involve small groups or individuals from the special class joining a regular class routinely for certain activities, such as greeting sessions, educational visits, or attending various community facilities, or for occasional events such as parties.

Social integration can provide a wider range of experiences in which children can practise their social skills. Research in America into the quantity and quality of interactions between children in mainstream settings as compared with those in segregated settings (Brinker and Thorpe, 1984) led the authors to conclude that although individual teaching of children with handicaps was necessary for the acquisition of skills, a variable social environment with their peers encouraged generalisation of the skills learned and had a positive effect on the children's achievement in their individual learning programmes. It would be unjustified to expect similar results from social integration of children with profound handicaps with their peers in regular classes within a school for children with severe learning difficulties. However, such integration allows them the opportunity to be part of a more cohesive group, with a richer flow of social interactions than is usual in a special class, and it permits them to practise their social skills with people in their own age group as well as with members of staff and their parents or carers at home.

Social interaction and the chance to build relationships with their peers, particularly in adolescence, is very important for children with profound handicaps who have some social competence in order to encourage social and emotional maturity. Even though members of the other classes in the school may be severely mentally handicapped, they will offer models of behaviour which are more age appropriate than those found in the wide age range of the special class and the expectations of behaviour will be closer to the generally accepted norm. For older children, in particular, joining their peer groups will reduce the likelihood of them being treated like infants, which can be a danger in a class which may span the whole of the school age range.

Children whose learning and social interaction skills are not sufficient to allow them to benefit from joining another class, can join the whole school at certain times. Being part of a large group of people with a common purpose, with the special atmosphere that this creates, can provide them with a positive experience even if they cannot participate actively. It also confirms acceptance by the school of all pupils as part of the corporate whole, regardless of their degree of handicap.

Some social integration on an individual basis is relatively easy to introduce in most school settings. For it to be successful members of staff must be aware of its purpose and be actively involved in promoting the process of this form of integration. Social integration inevitably takes place in less structured settings than most other school activities and much of the learning involved is incidental. Children with profound handicaps may need help to make the best use of the opportunities for interaction that exist.

FUNCTIONAL

Some children with multiple handicaps and special educational needs acquire the skills and learning strategies which make it both possible and desirable for them to participate in some, if not all, regular class activities, provided sufficient staff and resources are available to support them. They may join groups working at an appropriate level in various curriculum areas, or with a specialist teacher from whom the child can benefit but who might not be available to carry out teaching sessions in the special class.

The survey carried out by Evans and Ware (1987) showed that children with profound handicaps based in special classes rarely had an adequate functional system of communication. This aspect of the curriculum must, therefore, be a priority for the majority. Regular classes usually provide a richer verbal environment than the special class, both in terms of structured language use and informal situations where the exchanges are generated by the children themselves rather than the teachers. In their examination of the integration process Brady, McEvoy, Gunter, Shores, and Rox (1984) described various types of social behaviours which are appropriate to different settings. Transient responses, like greetings, are appropriate when sharing common areas such as corridors. More prolonged, reciprocal exchanges, like those involved in sharing materials, exchanging information, or participating in informal conversations, are appropriate during recreational activities. Children who are acting as helpers tend to show "accepting responses" towards their peers who are handicapped and can encourage them to participate in a wider range of social responses than usual.

Functional integration, therefore, offers a learning situation which requires some incidental learning. It also makes greater demands on the skills of children with profound handicaps and has higher expectations of their ability to achieve in areas of the curriculum which are not priorities in the special class. Outside of the special class, with fewer restrictions on children in terms of disability, there is an opportunity to acquire a wider range of skills and body of knowledge. This encourages a higher degree of competence and autonomy.

Certain general criteria should be fulfilled before full-time integration is considered. Children should show an understanding of familiar situations, social awareness, and a desire for interaction with their peers, and some effective learning strategies which will allow spontaneous learning to take place. Once these criteria are met there must be detailed consideration of their individual needs and capabilities and a programme of integration must be formulated. Fish (1985) states that "individually arranged integration always requires staffing allocation". This is true whether the integration takes place in mainstream education or in the special school.

For example, if a child joins a regular class for specific sessions each week accompanied by a member of staff, the same member of staff should accompany the child every time so that both can become accepted as members of the class group. This allows the support staff member to play a full part in the classroom team and it helps the class teacher to deploy her assistants in the most effective way.

Benefits for children in regular classes

The process of integration is certain to have some effect upon children from the host class. Although integration is undertaken primarily for the benefit of children with profound handicaps, it brings with it certain benefits for the regular class pupils. The opportunity to take responsibility for helping other people and understanding their needs is not often available to children with severe learning difficulties, who are more likely to be receiving such help themselves. The presence in the class of pupils with profound handicaps allows the more able children to form caring and understanding relationships with others more vulnerable than themselves. Not only can they learn when and how to help but, sometimes more difficult for them, they can learn to restrain themselves and encourage children from the special class to achieve things for themselves. Being more competent than others can increase the confidence and self-esteem of regular class children and lead them to a more positive assessment of their own abilities.

Another benefit is for less able members of the regular class who may themselves gain from the teaching methods and equipment used with the special class pupils, especially if the regular class teacher finds some of the resources and techniques useful and incorporates them into her own repertoire of teaching skills.

Integration as a two-way process

Integration is not necessarily one way. Although it is usually thought of as members of a special class joining the whole school or a regular class at various times for various purposes, children from the regular classes can also be integrated into the special class. Individual children or groups may use the special class resources: perhaps to work with someone with special expertise such as the physiotherapist; or to use special facilities such as a light room, soft play area, or therapy pool; or to enjoy a more protective environment than the school playground at playtime. Regular class children with additional handicaps may attend the special class for activities appropriate to their needs which cannot easily be provided in the regular classroom: to experience using free play materials — sand, water, clay, and paint — to encourage investigation or choice-making; or to benefit from certain movement activities carried out in the special class.

More able senior pupils from regular classes may join the special class, individually or in groups, to perform particular duties as part of their social skills curriculum. They may be asked to help in social activities, at mealtimes, or in educational activities. Although their role will be as helpers, supervision of these children will make more, rather than fewer, demands upon the staff and because of their status as colleagues this supervision and guidance must be carried out in a particularly subtle and sensitive way.

Time spent in a special class can be a very valuable part of a regular class member's individual programme. Opportunities for the special class to contribute to the school as a whole, in terms of functional integration, are easily overlooked. If integration is truly to be a two-way process, of value to all the children in the school, a well-planned timetable and a generous staffing level are essential. If the school's overall resources are not sufficient it may not be possible for integration to occur on a regular basis.

Integration is not necessarily an "all or none" situation. Locational and social integration are essentially sessional in their form. There will always be some children who will remain based in the special needs class but who will use the common facilities as a group, and join their contemporaries in regular classes at certain times for social or educational reasons. Some children will benefit from full integration and may be based in a regular class full-time as long as extra support is available at key periods. Others may be based in a regular class but be withdrawn during activities which are inappropriate for them when they can join sessions in the special class to supplement their regular class curriculum.

Placement in a regular class or the special class will depend to some extent upon availability of necessary support. If too many staff are providing support in the regular classrooms the number remaining in the special class may be depleted to such an extent that many children are deprived of attention for the sake of a few. The needs of children who are joining other classes must be carefully balanced with the needs of those who remain in the special class when planning the timetable.

A school which has a well-developed integration policy is likely to have a wide spectrum of arrangements to meet the needs of all its pupils and to make the best use of the resources of the school as a whole.

Contra-indications

There are some children for whom integration, other than locational, is not desirable. It is important to avoid making the assumption that integration is always beneficial. Loring and Burn (1975) point out that: "it is counterproductive and may be disastrous merely to mix or to integrate out of a vague desire not to leave anybody out . . .". This can increase a child's isolation and deprivation despite being physically present in the classroom. Fish (1985) describes handicap as a dynamic and relative concept, with the extent of the handicap at any given time depending upon the interaction between an individual's actual disabilities and the social contexts and the physical and educational situations in which that person is placed. The person's needs and abilities and the features of the environment must be compatible to make the process of integration successful.

Many children with profound handicaps will not have developed the basic skills and strategies necessary for effective learning; their needs cannot be met by the regular classroom and curriculum. Even use of the general school facilities will have to be carefully structured for each child individually. This will require careful assessment of the combination of each child's existing skills and educational needs, and the extent to which these can be met within a special class or in a regular class, in order to establish the type and amount of integration likely to be most successful and the additional resources that will be necessary.

One of the implications of the relative concept of handicap is that the characteristics of a host class might not be suitable for a child who is profoundly handicapped. The group dynamics might be such that great disruption could be caused in absorbing a new member with special needs into the class; or the physical conditions or behaviour of existing class members might put a particularly vulnerable child at risk. The regular class teacher may not be ready to accept a child with profound handicaps into the class, being concerned with the well-being of the existing pupils. The teacher may not appreciate how the new child can be included in classroom activities, or recognise the benefits which can be derived from the situation for everyone. If integration is used as an excuse for removing a child from the special class, with little thought about what the child is going to do or why, then such an attitude by the regular class teacher is justified. It could be that resources are insufficient to maintain the smooth running of the regular class, or to enable the child from the special class to benefit from inclusion in its activities.

Adequate consultation and careful planning will help to prevent situations of this kind from arising as many of these obstacles can be overcome. No integration policy will succeed, however, without the commitment of all the teachers involved and the provision of sufficient resources.

Integration within a single school

Establishing and carrying out a coherent policy for integration, which includes every child in the special classes to some extent, requires much discussion and planning on all levels and determination to overcome the obstacles, both great and small, which will inevitably arise. A structured network of support throughout the school (see Fig 6) will help to ensure smooth running of the integration scheme and the school as a whole.

The head of the school will define the school's overall integration policy, following consultation with school governors, parents, and members of staff. Discussion with everyone involved will: help to clarify the principles and criteria for implementing the policy; allay fears and convince those who are doubtful of the benefits; and enable planning of procedures and development of strategies to overcome difficulties. Decisions will have to be taken about the allocation of resources and appointment and development of staff within the school as a whole. Funds may be needed to supply extra resources for children from the special class who may need special arrangements whilst in other classes for toileting and personal hygiene, as well as educational aids and, possibly, large equipment such as special seating and work tables.

A senior member of the teaching staff, who has a broad area of responsibility within the school, might coordinate the scheme and assume overall responsibility for the children who join regular class groups. This will involve organisation of resources and facilities from the very general, such as ensuring that locational integration takes place and the special class has equal access to communal facilities, to the specific, for instance, ensuring that appropriate resources are available to cater for each child's individual needs. There will also be a need to negotiate with all the class teachers involved in order to coordinate the additional support that is required, both within and outside the classrooms, and to ensure that it is available when and where it is most needed and so can be used to the best advantage.

The regular class teachers are likely, at least in the beginning, to need someone with whom they can discuss the organisational problems which may occur and the educational programmes of the "integrated" children. The coordinating teacher may be able to offer this support directly, and be involved in detailed planning of individual or group teaching sessions. Alternatively, the coordinating teacher will ensure that advice and support is available from others who are experienced in teaching children with profound handicaps. Either way, the special class teacher must be involved in planning, with the regular class teachers, the programmes and activities that are to be carried out in regular classes with the children from the special class.

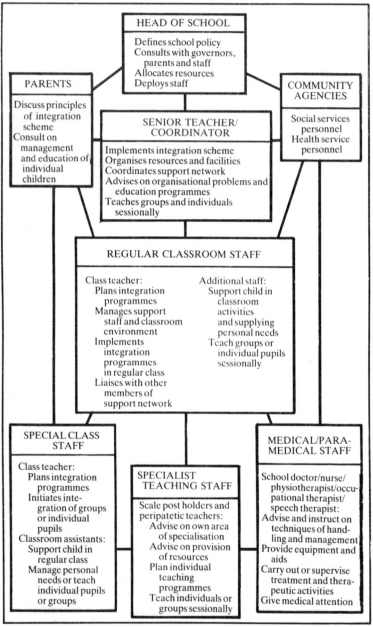

FIGURE 6. Network of support needed for integrating children with profound handicaps into regular classes

Many people will be involved in the support network at the classroom level. The special class teacher will often take the initiative in suggesting and implementing all forms of integration in the course of individual programme planning and daily timetabling for the special class. This teacher will be responsible for planning how the general school facilities will be used by children from the special class in their time-tabled sessions, and will be involved in planning the integration of groups and individuals into the other classes, whether on a full-time or sessional basis.

The individual aims of integration for every child must be agreed by all the teachers concerned. The amount of integration and the form it takes will depend upon each child's needs and the type of activities that take place in the regular classes. Assessment of each child's skills and educational needs, and the extent to which they can be met within a special class or in a regular class, is vital. Once it is agreed that integration is desirable it will have to be decided whether it should be full-time or sessional, and whether it will be for social or educational reasons. Objectives can then be discussed and support planned to enable the child to achieve these objectives in regular class settings. The early days of a child's integration must be particularly carefully organised. The child must be given time to settle in the new class and feel secure before being expected to start learning new skills and work towards educational objectives.

Planning of this kind demands an ability on the the part of each teacher to appreciate the views and priorities of other teachers and, where sessional integration is concerned, to cooperate closely in determining timetables for each child which will fit in with all the class routines.

There are several sources of support both within and outside the school. Specialist teachers for various curriculum areas can advise on the best ways of integrating children with profound handicaps in activities in their area of specialisation. Alternatively, they might set up special small group or individual sessions at an appropriate level. Peripatetic teachers for children with specific disabilities can advise on methods and equipment to facilitate learning and help to plan activities which can be carried out in the regular classroom. Para-medical staff, such as the speech therapist, physiotherapist, and occupational therapist, can advise on handling and management techniques and suggest appropriate aids and equipment, give regular treatment, or help to plan activities which will be therapeutic for individual children. The school doctor and nurse will advise the classroom staff on specific medical conditions and any resultant implications, such as precautions to be followed or action to be taken in different circumstances.

The greatest amount of personal and educational support in regular classes will be given to the children by classroom assistants who will probably be members of staff from the special class who know the children well. This is undoubtedly essential in the early stages while children are settling into the new group but once they are established the process can be taken over by members of the regular class team or by unattached staff whose role is to support children with profound handicaps in regular classes throughout the school. It is important, however, to provide consistency and so the same members of staff should provide the same children with support on each occasion and they should be well briefed on the objectives set for and the methods to be used with each child.

As more children with profound handicaps leave the special class to join other groups, the resources and facilities of that class will become more available for use by members of regular classes. If these facilities are to be offered to all pupils, however, a high staff ratio and generous resources, in terms of equipment and space, will be necessary. If these conditions pertain, the special class can be transformed from a backwater to become the hub of a planned and purposeful interaction with all classes in the school. It can, in effect become a resource centre, offering expertise and resources to all children with additional handicaps, whether mild or severe, in the way that the Warnock Committee (1978) suggested that some special schools might become resource centres for the support of teachers and the benefit of children with special needs being educated in mainstream schools.

Integration with mainstream education

The moves towards integration in the wider sphere of education make it all the more important for children with profound handicaps to be educated as far as possible alongside their peers within schools for children with severe learning difficulties rather than segregated in special classes. Special classes, instead of being isolated, should be seen as a central resource of the school. Then when integration of children into mainstream education is being considered, it will no longer be possible for children with profound handicaps to be excluded from consideration on the grounds that they need segregated self-contained provision.

Various models of integration are being introduced. They may involve whole classes from special schools being moved into local mainstream schools when space becomes available. Unless children with profound handicaps have already been integrated into regular classes, or provision has been made for special classes also to be accommodated in the mainstream schools, the effect on the special class pupils who remain in the original special school buildings could be disastrous. The smaller the group of children outside the mainstream of educational provision, the more restricted their educational experience is likely to be, and the more difficult it becomes to provide them with an education which fulfils the basic aims "to enlarge a child's knowledge, experience and understanding" which will allow that child to become a participant and contributor to society, "capable of achieving as much independence as possible".

Models for integration within a single school, similar to the one that has been described, are being implemented in some places, the schemes allowing classes, groups, or individual children to join their peer groups in local mainstream schools for planned sessions. Here again there is a danger, even if it is not quite so obvious, that children with profound handicaps may be excluded from the arrangements made for regular classes.

Whichever model is adopted, it is evident that much thought and forward planning must take place to solve the dilemma noted by Hurst (1983) "of providing special treatment for some individuals in a context where the emphasis is on equality and to avoid a retrograde step towards the extent of segregation suffered by many of these children prior to the moves towards community provision and education of children with severe learning difficulties in the 1970's". To prevent this situation from developing it is vital that there should be a well established scheme for integration of children with profound handicaps into the regular classes of schools for children with severe learning difficulties so that they too can share in further processes of integration and enjoy equal access to education in the community.

Stainback and Stainback (1984) comment that:

"with careful planning it should be possible to meet the unique needs of all students within one unified system of education — a system that does not deny differences but rather a system that recognises and accommodates for differences".

References

Brady, M. P., McEvoy, M. A., Gunter, P., Shores, R. E., Rox, J. J. Considerations for socially integrated school environments for severely handicapped students. *Educ. & Train. of the Ment. Retard.*, 1984; Dec., 246-253.

Brinker, R. P., Thorpe, M. E. Integration of severely handicapped students and the proportions of IEP objectives achieved. *Except. Child.*, 1984; **51**:2, 168-175.

Cotton, E. *Conductive education and cerebral palsy.* London: The Spastics Society, 1980.

Court Report. *Fit for the future. Report of the Committee on Child Health Services.* London: HMSO, 1976.

Department of Education and Science. *Special needs in education.* London: HMSO, 1980.

Education (Handicapped Children) Act, 1970. London: HMSO, 1970.

Education Act, 1981. London: HMSO, 1981.

Evans, P. L., Ware, J. *Special Care Provision: the education of children with profound and multiple learning difficulties.* Windsor: NFER/Nelson, 1987.

Fish Report. *Equal Opportunities for All? Report of the Committee reviewing provision to meet special educational needs.* London: ILEA, 1985.

Hurst, A. Legislating for special education. *Spec. Educ. Forward Trends*, 1983; **11**:1, 6-9.

Loring, J., Burn, G. *Integration of Handicapped Children in Society.* London: Routledge and Kegan Paul, 1975.

Mental Health Act, 1983. London: HMSO, 1983.

Ouvry, C. Integrating pupils with profound and multiple handicaps in a school for children with severe learning difficulties. *Ment. Hand.*, 1986; **14**:4, 157-160.

Stainback, S., Stainback, S. A rationale for the merger of special and regular education. *Except. Child.*, 1984; **51**:2, 102-111.

Warnock Committee, The. *The Special educational needs: Report of the Committee of Enquiry into the Education of Handicapped Children and Young People (Warnock Report.).* Cmnd. 7212. London: HMSO, 1978.

Part 2

Educational aims for
children with profound handicaps
and a curriculum model
to meet their needs

Introduction

It is still often thought, by people in education as well as other professions, that children with profound handicaps do not learn and, by implication, cannot be taught; and that activities carried out in the special class are therefore confined to caring, containment or, at best, general stimulation and entertainment of both pupils and staff. This belief denies the possibility of long-term aims for the children and the value of constructing individual programmes for them in order to promote progress towards predetermined goals. It has the effect of devaluing and deskilling the teachers and classroom assistants who work in the special class.

An over-emphasis on care can result in staff being placed in special classes who are motherly and caring but who do not always have the skills necessary to carry out a timetable which is intellectually rigorous and physically demanding. Although many pupils in the special class do not learn spontaneously in situations where incidental learning might be expected to take place, this is not because they are unable to learn in all circumstances but because the nature of their disabilities creates such obstructions to learning that acquisition of new skills does not take place without carefully planned and consistent teaching.

As well as receiving restricted or distorted information as a result of sensory or physical handicaps, many of the children have not developed the strategies and mental processes which are fundamental to learning. These basic skills, which enable them to interact with and organise their environment, must be acquired before progress in more obvious ways can be expected. Organising and performing actions to achieve the desired results can be major causes of difficulty for the children, and can prevent them from exercising control over their surroundings and experiences. Feedback from unsuccessful actions can cause children to become frustrated and lead to withdrawal from the situation, or it can result in them indulging in bizarre or stereotyped behaviours.

These problems have been discussed more fully in Part 1, Chapter 2. The remainder of the book attempts to relate these issues to the planning and implementation of a coherent and balanced curriculum which offers activities and experiences which are relevant to all pupils with profound handicaps, both as individuals and as members of a group. A heirarchy of aims is identified which creates the ethical and philosophical background, establishes the general direction of the curriculum, and enables the setting of goals for individual pupils. It is suggested that the ultimate aim for all children should be the greatest possible degree of autonomy and self-determination that is compatible with the limitations imposed on them by the nature of their disabilities. This aim sets the direction of every child's education.

Lack of learning strategies and absence of incidental learning makes the need for structured teaching particularly important for pupils with profound and multiple learning difficulties. There has been a great emphasis in recent years on the importance of individual programmes in the teaching of these pupils. Such programmes often concentrate on activities which are undertaken in a one-to-one teaching situation and aim for specific behavioural objectives. They usually exclude group activities, or those with social or expressive objectives. A balanced and integrated curriculum model which provides a unifying structure is therefore essential to ensure that all aspects of the children's development are covered. Without such a structure individual teaching programmes are likely to result in the acquisition of isolated skills and fragmented learning which will be of little practical use to the children. The curriculum must provide a range of activities and experiences which will enable children not only to acquire new skills but also to practise and use those skills in a variety of situations. The individual programmes designed for the children should each provide a continuous sequence of experiences which includes every activity in the school day. Each experience should offer some potential for learning or consolidation of acquired skills, whether undertaken in a more or less structured setting.

The following chapters describe a curriculum model in which the core areas contribute towards four major developmental areas. The core areas are discussed and their components are given in detail. Some activities which can be used within the component areas are outlined. The model forms a unifying structure for pupils' programmes, and makes it possible to plan and implement programmes for individual children within a curriculum which caters for the group as a whole.

The process of planning individual programmes for use within the curriculum model is discussed. There is a need for some form of assessment upon which to base this planning and a way of achieving an initial profile of each child's skills and deficits, based upon observation, is set out in Appendix 1. Various other assessments and checklists are currently available (some of which are listed in Appendix 3 on page 205) which can substitute for or supplement the initial profile suggested.

The objectives identified in children's individual programmes, whether behavioural or expressive, will suggest activities which would be appropriate in working towards these objectives. Monitoring of progress is essential, and examples of various forms are included which are suitable for monitoring different types of activity. Periodic recording based on informal observations will be quite adequate for some activities, whereas rigorous monitoring of every response may be necessary for others. A method of recording activities in the second category is illustrated.

Teachers are not only responsible for planning and implementing educational programmes. They must also consider the relationship of education, therapy, and care, as well as the respective roles of teacher, therapist, and classroom assistant. The sharing of expertise is as essential as the role of teachers in coordinating activities into meaningful experiences for the children. Teachers must establish a close working relationship with the parents or carers of their pupils and the many other professionals who might be involved with them, both within and outside of school.

CHAPTER 5

Aims of education for children with profound handicaps

Since April 1971, when the provisions of the 1970 *Education (Handicapped Children) Act* were implemented, all children have been the responsibility of education authorities. In order to justify the time, effort, and expense of educational provision for children with profound handicaps there must be a qualitative difference between their experiences in training centres or hospitals prior to 1971 and their experiences in schools since then.

In regular classrooms of schools for children with severe learning difficulties this difference can be observed, not only in the activities which make up the curriculum but also in the methods used to teach the children and, equally important, in the aims and objectives which determine curriculum content and educational techniques. The aims of education, as outlined in this Chapter, and progress towards those aims can readily be seen. However, children with profound handicaps are so severely limited, and their progress is so slow, that it is all too easy to lose sight of the overall aims of education and revert to "training" in areas in which some practical achievement can be seen. But the purpose of the 1970 *Act* was to widen the experience of these children and to give them the same opportunity as other children to benefit from educational approaches and methods which seek more for them than just learning skills, important though this may be, and which is concerned with what each child is, not just how that child behaves.

What is education?

The concept of education is very wide. It may include all aspects of rearing or bringing up children, wherever this may take place; or, as in this book, it may refer to more specific processes which occur in certain contexts and for which certain criteria have to be met to justify the term education. This more restricted definition refers to the teaching processes and activities which occur, in or out of school, as part of a planned programme although it is recognised that much learning, which could justify the term education, takes place in more informal ways.

Universal aims

Hirst and Peters (1970) suggest that the concept of education includes a family of activities which implies ends and means. The ends are normative, embodying the characteristics of the person being educated and specifying the aims of education. The means specify the processes which are believed to lead towards or achieve those aims. It is, therefore, necessary to state the aims of education before the means can be determined. The normative aspects of education give rise to statements of aims in both general and specific terms.

Broad aims of education employ concepts such as self-realisation and self-actualisation which involve:

> "the maximum development of abilities and skills of which the individual is capable" (Hutt and Gibby, 1976);

or use phrases such as:

> "complete social, physical and emotional development" (Leeming, Swann, Coupe, and Mittler, 1979); or:
> "all round preparation for life" (Tansley and Gulliford, 1960).

These statements have the virtue that they are universally applicable to all children, regardless of their capabilities or limitations, and apply to all ages and stages of development. They emphasise the fact that education is appropriate and justifiable for all children. Kiernan, Jordan, and Saunders (1978) state unequivocally that:

> "to be educated according to whatever capabilities he may have is a child's right as a human being".

Such broad statements, however, are not particularly helpful in specifying aims for individual children or even groups of children and, as the *Plowden Report* (1966) points out:

> "general statements of aims tend to be little more than expressions of benevolent aspiration which may provide a rough guide to the general climate of the school, but which may have a rather tenuous relationship to the educational practices that actually go on there".

This does not mean to say that they are valueless for it is important to establish the ethical and philosophical basis for education. This is particularly true in times when funding for education has to compete with other areas of public expenditure which have equally compelling reasons for the allocation of resources.

General aims

If the aims are to be useful in determining the content and methods of education, the ends must be stated in more definite terms than abstractions such as "fulfilment" and "self-realisation". Educational aims must describe the hoped-for state of individuals at the end of the educational process. The general direction and priorities to be placed upon the many activities which education embraces can then be determined.

The Warnock Committee (1978) suggested that the aims of education should be:

> "to enlarge a child's knowledge, experience and understanding and thus his or her awareness of moral values and capacity for enjoyment";

and that the child should become:

> "an active participant in society and a responsible contributor to it, capable of achieving as much independence as possible".

Hirst and Peters (1970) have suggested that there are two conditions, desirability and knowledge, which education seeks to promote. Desirability refers to the normative aspects of education. Society's assumptions of what characteristics are desirable in adults determine the "ideal" towards which children are guided. This ideal is not only specific to the society which determines it, but varies according to the values of different groups within that society. The main emphasis is upon children as members of society. Knowledge refers to children's understanding and their ability to derive meaning from and to use their experiences. The emphasis is upon depth and breadth of understanding rather than narrow, specialised skills and knowledge. It is this which distinguishes education from training. The condition places emphasis on children as individuals and is concerned as much with what they are as with what they do.

These two conditions, which will now be discussed, are helpful when considering the aims of education for children with severe learning difficulties, namely that:

> "the general aims of special educational treatment are substantially the same as for any other children. Any

differences that exist are chiefly a matter of emphasis to be placed on particular aims" (Tansley and Gulliford, 1960).

THE DESIRABILITY CONDITION

The desirability condition describes the skills and qualities which will enable individuals to operate effectively and make a positive contribution towards society, in whatever sphere this may be. In order to specify these skills and qualities some account must be taken of the nature and demands of the future situation as far as it can be known and the qualities which will be relevant and effective. This is true for all children, with or without handicaps. The fact that children with profound handicaps will always require an environment which is modified to take account of their handicaps, and awareness that the extent to which they will be able to operate effectively will be severely limited, does not in any way alter the general aims for them. These factors, however, will influence the specific aims set for each child and the extent of progress that can be accomplished.

The emphasis of education for children who are not handicapped, is upon achieving certain personal, educational, and behavioural standards which will ensure that they can support themselves independently in the community and make a positive contribution towards society. Children with handicaps do not undergo the same pressure to conform to the demands of society; their educational aims not being set in terms of what is normal and useful, but in terms of what is desirable for them as individuals. Normalisation, which enables these children to participate as freely as possible in the community, is a desirable goal; but it does not necessarily have the same priority for every child. Subjective decisions about what is desirable for children with profound handicaps have to be made by those responsible for making physical provision and setting educational aims. It is generally assumed that it is desirable for them to develop skills and qualities which will be useful and appropriate in the future, and which will enable them to exercise the greatest possible degree of personal independence and allow them the fullest possible participation in and maximum benefit from their physical and social environment.

Autonomy is one of the most frequently cited aims for children who are not handicapped, and Dearden (1968) has described it as consisting of self-direction, self-activity, independence, and being "a chooser". He suggests that in achieving autonomy there is a shift in emphasis from a situation in which the initiative comes from the teacher to a situation in which the initiative comes from the child. Although the physical and mental limitations of children with profound handicaps make these goals exceptionally difficult to achieve, they summarise the essential characteristics of the desirability condition for these children in every aspect of life. Leeming, Swann, Coupe, and Mittler (1979) suggested that autonomy can conveniently be regarded as the ultimate aim in every curriculum area; and that it will determine the more specific aims in these areas. Transfer of responsibility from adults and caretakers to the children themselves will enhance those children's social, emotional, physical, and intellectual development, help to create in them a positive self-concept, and thus ensure that their contribution to society, however small, is a positive one.

THE KNOWLEDGE CONDITION

The knowledge condition referred to by Hirst and Peters (1970) also contributes towards the autonomy of individuals:

"to know is to have a sense of mastery which is basic to the sense of confidence in oneself".

This knowledge need not be in the form of specific skills and abilities but can embrace a general awareness and understanding of the human and natural environment which enables children to use their skills and abilities in appropriate ways and thus exercise some control over their own lives.

Brennan (1974) has described two forms of learning which promote the knowledge condition. The first is learning for thoroughness, and this is necessary in areas where permanent and accurate understanding and skills are required to enable children to operate effectively in their immediate environment. However, Brennan warns that the "content limitations required to achieve quality of learning in the basic subjects" can result in programmes which are "arid, repetitive, lacking in excitement and in transfer outside the school situation". These restrictions, Brennan suggests, can be counter-balanced by promoting breadth of understanding through the second form of learning which he has elaborated from Tansley and Gulliford's (1960) concept of "education for awareness". This Brennan describes as a familiarity with the mainstream of human experience and with the social framework of the society in which the child lives.

It is the experiences which underlie this familiarity which are frequently denied to children with profound handicaps because of their physical and intellectual limitations. The knowledge condition in children without handicaps is promoted by extending their abilities and broadening their educational experiences. Education for children with profound handicaps must aim not only to build upon and extend their abilities and experiences but also to compensate for the deficits which result from the restrictions imposed by their disabilities. Tansley and Gulliford (1960) consider that:

"this is not merely an agreeable addition to the basic curriculum but (it) makes an essential contribution to it".

The conditions of desirability and knowledge, coupled with the concepts of education for thoroughness and education for awareness, are useful in defining the aims applicable to different groups of children. In their study of the aims considered to be most important by parents and teachers of pupils with handicaps, Leeming, Swann, Coupe, and Mittler (1979) found that both groups rated highly independence, social relations, and emotional stability. These correspond well with the desirability and knowledge conditions in leading to the effective action and self-determination that is necessary to achieve autonomy and control of the environment. Such aims are appropriate for everyone, whether handicapped or not.

The general aims of education provide a structure within which specific aims for individual children can be identified. These specific aims will determine children's individual programmes and the curriculum areas, activities, and teaching methods which will be selected. If the aims are to be realistic and appropriate to children's capabilities and life-style, a preliminary assessment of every child must be made to establish each one's current level of functioning in all areas and to identify the main obstructions to learning. Appendix 1 offers a guide which can be used to compile an initial profile for each child which will highlight these two aspects. The completed profile will give some indication of the progress which might reasonably be expected and, together with information on the opportunities which will be open after leaving school, will suggest aims which are relevant for the children both in the present and for the future. Although these will be only tentative conclusions, which must be changed whenever they are shown to be inaccurate, they can provide the starting point from which individual programmes can be planned.

Specific aims

It is important to identify specific aims for each child in all developmental areas in order to ensure a balanced and integrated educational programme and to avoid fragmentation of learning. Specific aims within the four major developmental areas of movement, perception, intellectual development, and social competence are set out in Appendix 2. These can be used to suggest appropriate aims for individual children.

When setting specific aims for children it is essential to consider them both as members of society and as individuals in their own right. If children are to be welcome in the community certain characteristics are desirable. Acceptable behaviour and appearance are among the most important, since they create an initial impression which can have a lasting effect upon subsequent relationships, experiences, and opportunities. The extent of children's integration with the wider community will ultimately depend upon how well they can function in relation to their social and physical environment.

The degree of autonomy that can be achieved by children who are profoundly handicapped is small. Self-help and social skills must be a priority for them because these can preserve their dignity and ease the management and handling problems which result from their disabilities. Even if they make good progress in acquiring these skills, they will remain highly dependent upon their care-takers, whether at home, in day centres, or in residential accommodation. When adult, their physical management can be extremely taxing on care-takers, so it is very important to help the children to lessen their dependency as much as possible. Participation in their own personal care may extend only as far as learning to tolerate handling and cooperating with others; or it may progress as far as being able to transfer or take their own weight, or to carry out specific self-help skills.

Every effort should be made to encourage children to be responsive, cheerful, and cooperative. They will then be easier to manage and more pleasant to help and to be with. This can result in them enjoying a better physical, social, and emotional quality of life.

Self-determination, however, can take forms other than exercising self-help skills. Even the most physically dependent children can be helped to understand their surroundings and to acquire strategies for control of their immediate environment. By learning to accept the consequences of their own actions they can begin to make decisions which will influence their own experiences, and thus take responsibility for themselves in a limited way.

Gardner (1969) speaks of planned dependence and points out that people who are severely handicapped must be educated not only to be acceptable and as competent as possible within a situation of dependence, but must also be educated for leisure rather than vocational aims. This concept is no longer only applicable to people whose limitations preclude them from competing for paid employment in the open market, the age of technology and the present economic climate changing employment expectations and the amount of leisure time available for many people, regardless of handicap. It is important, however, for children with profound handicaps to acquire skills and interests which will enable them to occupy themselves in an acceptable manner, but their ability to do this and so to participate in and enjoy social and leisure activities will rest upon the attainment of knowledge and understanding.

It is difficult, when considering the knowledge condition for individual children, to define specific aims because the outcome is a state of being, rather than a cluster of observable characteristics, which must take into account each one's capabilities. Consideration must be given to what Campione and Brown (1977) differentiated as mental structures, which are relatively unmodifiable, and control processes, which are children's habitually used strategies for learning or operating that are subject to modification through teaching, as well as the influences on children of their present environment and their previous experiences.

Decisions as to how children's capabilities can be developed to enable them to operate effectively and exercise the highest degree of autonomy compatible with their limitations will have to take account of their probable future situation. It is counter-productive for children to spend long periods learning inappropriate skills which they will be unable to use later. This is not to say that the curriculum must be tailor-made for the future which is often, regrettably, spent in less than ideal conditions but priority should be given to teaching skills and abilities which will enable individuals to participate in and make the most of their situation.

Handicap has been described as dynamic, relative to the expectations of others and the social contexts to which individuals are subject (Fish, 1985). This concept implies that the aims of education should be informed not only by examining and increasing children's skills and understanding in relation to their environment, but also by examining and possibly changing their environment if this is contributing to their degree of handicap.

In working towards a knowledge condition the aim must be to make good the deficits as far as possible. This means encouraging the acquisition of effective learning strategies and a repertoire of skills for use in all situations. These must be learned with thoroughness if children are to be able to select, integrate, and derive meaning from their experiences. Autonomy in the children's use of skills should be developed so that they are not just exercises carried out with adults but are transferred and used appropriately in other circumstances, thus allowing the children a degree of control over their environment. Understanding of their environment is essential if children are to be able to make judgements about appropriate behaviour and so exercise their independence in an acceptable way.

The restricted experience of the children, which results from their physical and intellectual limitations, compounds the effects of their deficits. Attempts should be made to compensate for this by increasing their knowledge and understanding of the environment. Education for awareness must provide varied but carefully planned experiences. Activities undertaken should link with and reinforce each other rather than provide isolated experiences which have no relevance to daily life inside or outside school. They will then help children to develop an awareness and appreciation of the social framework in which they are to live and participate.

It is extremely important, when considering the specific aims for individual children, to consult with parents or carers and to take into account their priorities in relation to the children. This will ensure that the programmes devised will be seen to be relevant, not just in terms of the school curriculum, but also in relation to the children's home lives.

Hierarchy of aims

The aims of education may be considered as a hierarchy (see Figure 7), each level becoming more explicit in the outcome which it seeks to promote.

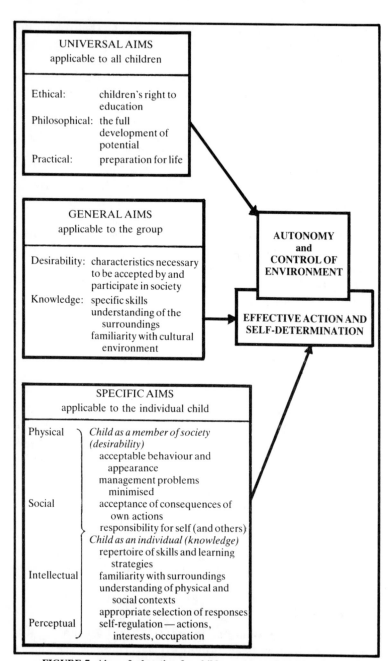

FIGURE 7. Aims of education for children with profound handicaps

Universal aims refer to abstractions, such as total individual development, and preparation for and quality of life, which are applicable to everyone regardless of age, ability, or background. They set the ethical and philosophical background for education but do not specify the conditions through which it can be achieved.

General aims are more explicit, referring to the conditions of desirability and knowledge which education should promote. They are applicable to groups of children. Desirability refers to development of the characteristics considered necessary if children are to make a positive contribution to society in adulthood. It reflects the social, political, and cultural environment. Knowledge is seen in terms of breadth and depth of understanding, rather than instrumental knowledge in specific areas. General aims to promote these two conditions can be defined within each curriculum area. These will influence the choice of curriculum for specific groups of children and the means of implementing it.

Finally, specific aims refer to the concepts of desirability and knowledge as they relate to individual children. They are used at this level to determine the content and balance of the curriculum for each child, to set individual objectives, and devise appropriate teaching programmes.

It can be difficult to envisage general educational aims for children with profound handicaps. Aims for these children are frequently stated only at the specific level or in terms of behavioural objectives. Efforts should be made to overcome this situation and to establish an overall view of the aims of education for this group. This is essential if it is to be ensured that the educational programme for children with profound handicaps is not fragmented. By taking into account children as they are at present, and how and where they are likely to be in future, it will be possible to plan activities that are appropriate, coordinated, and relevant in the wider community throughout all periods of their school life.

References

Brennan, W. K. *Shaping the Education of Slow Learners*. London: Routledge and Kegan Paul, 1974.

Campione, J. C., Brown, A. L. Memory and metamemory development in educable retarded children. *In* Kail, R. V., Hagan, J. W. (Eds.). *Perspectives on the Development of Memory and Cognition*. New York: Laurence Erlbaum Assoc., 1977.

Dearden, R. F. *The Philosophy of Primary Education.* London: Routledge and Kegan Paul, 1968.

Education (Handicapped Children) Act, 1970. London: HMSO, 1970.

Fish Report. *Equal Opportunities for All? The Report of the Committee Reviewing Provision to Meet Special Educational Needs.* London: ILEA, 1985.

Gardner, L. Planning for planned dependence. *Spec. Educ.: Forward Trends, 1969;* **58**, 27-30.

Hirst, P. H., Peters, R. S. *The Logic of Education.* London: Routledge and Kegan Paul, 1970.

Hutt, M. L., Gibby, R. G. *The Mentally Retarded Child: development, education and treatment (3rd edn.).* Allyn Bacon Inc. Distrib. Hemel Hempstead: Prentice-Hall, 1976.

Kiernan, C., Jordan, R., Saunders, C. *Starting Off.* London: Souvenir Press, 1978.

Leeming, K., Swann, W., Coupe, J., Mittler, P. *Teaching Language and Communication to the Mentally Handicapped. (Schools Council Curriculum Bulletin 8).* London: Evans/Methuen Educational, 1979.

Plowden Report. *Children and Their Primary Schools: Report of the Central Advisory Council for Education.* London: HMSO, 1966.

Tansley, A. E., Gulliford, R. *The Education of Slow Learning Children.* London: Routledge and Kegan Paul, 1960.

Warnock Committee, The. *Special Educational Needs: Report of the Committee of Enquiry into the Education of Handicapped Children and Young People. (Warnock Report.)* Cmnd. 7212. London: HMSO, 1978.

CHAPTER 6

Education, therapy, or care?

Special classes for children with profound handicaps are known by many different names (Evans and Ware, 1987) but "special care" is still the most common and most generally understood name.

The special care class is often regarded, if not by the staff working in it, by those who work in the rest of the school, as precisely what its name implies: a unit where the children are cared for, where they may have some form of therapy or other specialised medical provision, but where education as such cannot take place because of the limitations imposed by their disabilities. This impression is all too easily incorporated into the attitudes of people who have no direct contact with the children; and, unfortunately it can even influence the approach of those who work closely with them. But care alone caters for only the most obvious of the children's needs.

A survey of 12 schools (Ouvry, 1983) showed that the staffing in special classes reflected three approaches: education, therapy, and care.

As far as education is concerned, there was usually one teacher for every special class, but the teacher:child ratio varied greatly and rarely, if ever, corresponded to any official recommendation.

In terms of therapy every school had the support of a physiotherapist for a varying number of sessions, part of whose time was available to the special class, but the number of sessions did not seem to relate in any way to the number of children with physical problems. The services of an occupational therapist were available in 75 per cent of the schools, but visits tended to be less regular. A survey by Evans and Ware (1986) shows that most occupational therapists visit schools only monthly or even less often. Speech therapists visited all schools regularly but their support in the special class was usually directed towards eating and drinking problems, rather than advising on the communication curriculum or individual programmes for developing communication skills. As the vast majority of children in special classes have little or no functional communication, greater support by speech therapists in this area would surely be of benefit.

Finally, with regard to care, by far the largest number of adults present in the special class were classroom assistants, who traditionally represent the "caring" function of the class. Their presence reflects the degree of dependence of the children.

It is vital, because of the number of people with different expertise involved, that everyone in the special class should work as a team, with a common philosophy and agreed goals. This necessitates a high degree of planning and cooperation to ensure that a balanced curriculum, in which education, therapy, and care each have their place, is provided for the children.

Maslow (1955) has distinguished two categories of need which must be supplied: deficit needs, which are the basic necessities for health and well-being; and growth needs, which are necessary for children's overall physical, intellectual, social, and emotional development. These are useful concepts when considering the relative roles of education, therapy, and care in the provision made for children with profound or multiple handicaps. They show that, despite the considerably limited level of achievement attainable by these children when measured against their non-handicapped peers, it is only through a programme in which all three approaches are integrated and tailored to the needs of individual children that all the requirements of each child's physical and mental development can be met. It is essential, therefore, that everyone working with the children should be aware of, and respect, the different functions and expertise of their colleagues and, especially, how the particular roles interact and complement each other.

Education

Education is concerned with the child as a whole. Unlike care, its principal function is not to supply the basic needs of the child, although it does not disregard these; unlike therapy, it does not concentrate on one aspect of the child. The aims of education are therefore very wide and can apply to all children regardless of their capabilities, even though:

> "the starting points are diverse, the speed and direction of growth will vary, and the destination will be even more diverse" (Schools Council Working Paper 70, 1981).

In ordinary schools education supplies the growth needs of the children and, starting with the capabilities they bring with them, builds upon and extends their physical, intellectual, and social skills. In our school system as it is, educational aims are determined by society's assumptions of the characteristics that are desirable in adults and growth is expected to proceed towards those characteristics.

In the education of children with multiple and profound handicaps it is fortunate that aims do not have to be set in terms of what is "normal", but in terms of what is desirable for individual children. Inevitably, however, aims for these children must include a degree of normalisation. The major difference in educational aims for this group is that not only must education provide for the children's growth needs, but it must also supply the deficit needs that arise from their poverty of experience.

FUNCTIONS FOR CHILDREN WITH PROFOUND HANDICAPS

Education for children with profound handicaps has, therefore, two functions. First, it must attempt to compensate for the limitations imposed upon children through their disabilities, by offering them experiences of all kinds. Each of these experiences must be carefully planned so that they have meaning for the children and can be linked to other experiences. Professor Hirst (1969) points out that:

> "provision of experience in itself is quite inadequate for developing even the simplest body of concepts".

If this is true of intact children, how much more true must it be of children with profound handicaps whose ability to select, organise, and integrate their experiences is impaired?

Secondly, education must seek to extend children's abilities, and their knowledge and understanding of the world around them. The educational curriculum must be devised to enable children to develop skills which will be relevant and useful to them, both in a practical sense and in their intellectual, social, and emotional development. It must also offer carefully selected and planned activities to encourage children to organise and integrate their experiences and to form the network of relationships which is the basis of cognitive development upon which understanding of their environment depends.

The class teacher is responsible for planning the curriculum for pupils as a group, as well as the day-to-day education of each individual child. Part of the teacher's role is to ensure that education, therapy, and care are coordinated so that each one reinforces the experiences of the other and every child in the class follows an integrated programme which caters for "the whole person".

Therapy

The high incidence of additional physical disabilities means that many children with profound handicaps require some form of therapy, usually provided by physio-, occupational, and speech therapists. Although the term therapy implies some form of correction to restore normal function, in the special class it has a much wider connotation. Therapy applies not only to the deficit needs created by the children's handicapping conditions, but also to their growth needs. In so doing it overlaps and contributes to both care and education to a considerable extent. Therapists must therefore be prepared to practise the skills of caring and education as well as their own specialist expertise and techniques.

PHYSIOTHERAPISTS

Most physiotherapists have other commitments in community or hospital settings and are able to spend relatively little time in schools for children with severe learning difficulties. An informal survey carried out in 15 schools in 10 health districts in London by members of the ILEA Working Party for Profoundly Handicapped Pupils, showed no correlation between the number of children with additional physical or medical conditions and the time allocated to physiotherapists in schools. The traditional model of treatment leading to improvement, if not cure, is not valid in the school setting, and nor does the segregated treatment session fit with the holistic approach of education. Physiotherapists are important members of the classroom team. As much of their time is likely to be spent elsewhere, however, they must rely upon other team members to follow their directions in carrying out individual programmes, using handling and management techniques which are appropriate for each child.

Physiotherapy programmes aim to correct, as far as possible, any deformities or dysfunctions resulting from the physical condition of the children. More importantly, they seek to prevent the development of any additional deformities or loss of function which would seriously impede their ability to participate in caring and educational activities. For those who have the responsibility of providing day-to-day care, preventing contractures and maintaining mobility of the limbs and trunk is vitally important as it affects the ease with which handling of the children and management of tasks such as dressing, hygiene, and movement can be carried out. As children grow bigger, these practical considerations assume even greater importance.

Physiotherapists can also encourage children's use of normal movement patterns and the development of voluntary motor control, at the same time discouraging abnormal movement patterns which may have a detrimental effect on their health and functioning. By encouraging functional, self-initiated movement the physiotherapy programme can contribute towards children's growth needs, not only directly through the development of motor skills but also by enabling children to participate in and derive maximum benefit from other activities which form part of the curriculum.

Individual physiotherapy programmes need to be planned in consultation with other members of the classroom team and carried out in a variety of ways and situations. Physiotherapists can advise on: correct handling and appropriate positioning, which will apply in every situation throughout the day; beneficial patterns of movement, which can be incorporated into many group or individual activities in other curriculum areas; and specific therapeutic techniques, which can be carried out in time-tabled individual sessions either by the physiotherapists themselves or by other members of staff under their guidance.

In most schools for children with profound handicaps physiotherapy is a scare resource; and where there are too many children with additional impairments for probably only one or two physiotherapists to work with personally, their role must be largely advisory, being concentrated on instructing and guiding other members of staff. This is extremely important. It increases the knowledge and skill of all the staff in the team and makes the greatest possible use of the physiotherapists' special expertise.

Finally, because of the physical demands upon the staff in the special class, physiotherapists have a vital role in advising on techniques for lifting and moving the children which will minimise the risk of strain and injury to the staff while carrying out these duties.

OCCUPATIONAL THERAPISTS

Occupational therapists can also enhance the work of teaching staff in many aspects of children's education. Sadly in many schools their role is restricted, because of lack of time, to advising on the practicalities involved in care and education. Occupational therapists can advise on suitable aids and equipment for use with individual children. Some of these, such as wheelchairs, feeding and bath aids, clothing, and safety devices such as padding, straps, or supports of various kinds, will ease the tasks of daily management and care; some, such as special seating, wedges, and standing frames, and adaptations of ordinary equipment, can improve children's functioning by providing security, stability, comfort, and a firm base from which they can exercise their abilities; and some, such as head pointers and electronic devices, will extend the children's own range of function and increase the effectiveness of their responses in specific situations. Occupational therapists, therefore, can contribute towards the deficit needs of the children by reducing problems of care and management, and to their growth needs by ensuring that they make the best possible use of their faculties and operate in the most effective way they can.

Occupational therapists need not be confined to advising on, supplying, or adapting aids. The majority of children in special classes have poor fine motor control and experience great difficulty in carrying out self-help and perceptual motor activities successfully. Occupational therapists can devise and carry out programmes for increasing children's personal independence in eating and drinking, washing, and dressing, as well as for helping them to acquire motor skills which will enhance their perceptual abilities and contribute towards their ability to communicate. They may thus be involved in many curriculum areas.

It is particularly regrettable, in view of their wide range of expertise, that regular occupational therapy sessions are available in relatively few schools, and most schools have access to occupational therapists on a very irregular basis, which prevents expansion of their role beyond the giving of advice on aids and equipment.

SPEECH THERAPISTS

Speech therapists are often less closely involved in the special class curriculum for children with profound handicaps than with that for the rest of the pupils in the regular classrooms (Ouvry, 1983). As most children in the special class are non-verbal, and few are likely to acquire much functional speech, speech therapists' expertise is seen as being more effectively used elsewhere.

Nevertheless, speech therapists can contribute, either directly or indirectly, to both the deficit and the growth needs of children with profound handicaps. They can, for example, assist in feeding programmes. This may involve showing staff how to employ special techniques to improve tongue and lip control or advising them about desensitisation routines, all of which can help children to overcome difficulties in eating and drinking and become more acceptable table companions.

Their specialist knowledge and advice is invaluable to teachers developing the communication curriculum for the class, helping them ensure that it is coordinated with language development programmes throughout the school. Their expertise in language development and alternative communication systems is of great benefit to teachers attempting to devise individual communication programmes suited to the existing abilities of their pupils. Rather than trying to develop conventional speech, the therapists are likely to recommend appropriate sign or symbol systems, and offer advice on introducing them to the children.

It is clear, therefore, that even if speech therapists rarely work directly with individual children or groups from the special class, they have an important contribution to make.

JOINT CONTRIBUTION

It can be seen from the preceding paragraphs that physio-, occupational, and speech therapy each has a role to play in meeting the needs which arise as a result of the disabilities of children with profound handicaps. All three therapies can contribute significantly to children's ability to benefit from teaching programmes.

It is essential that all three be regarded as part of the total curriculum for the development of fragmentary skills is of little benefit to the children. The general aim of all the professionals in the school must therefore be the same, and objectives must be planned to complement rather than counteract each other. Whenever possible therapy should be carried out in the teaching areas so that all members of staff know what treatment each child is receiving and can reinforce it in other activities. In this way therapy techniques can be integrated within children's individual programmes and any special sessions can be timetabled appropriately so that they enhance rather than detract from the overall educational programme.

Physio-, occupational, and speech therapists each have a very specialised knowledge and expertise compared with that of teachers and classroom assistants whose skills must embrace the whole range of curriculum activities. Their advice and support is invaluable to teachers who must carry out activities in those particular areas of specialisation, as well as being useful in general curriculum development. It is very important that therapists are willing to share their knowledge and expertise, and that teachers and classroom assistants are willing to accept and implement their advice for the benefit of the children.

Liaising with parents and home visiting are frequently seen as being an important part of the work of physio- and occupational therapists. It is common for parents to have particular confidence in the benefits of these kinds of therapy, whereas they may not appreciate the role of education in their children's development to the same extent. Therapists, therefore, may be well placed to introduce educational ideas and methods into the home as part of the integrated approach to the children, thus extending the children's opportunities for learning.

Care

Children with profound handicaps are dependent on a high degree of care to meet their physical and emotional needs. Without physical care they would not survive. Without emotional care their lives would be impoverished. Care, then, involves supplying the necessities for a healthy existence, both physical and psychological — the deficit needs described by Maslow (1955). Physical needs include food, warmth, hygiene, and protection from discomfort and danger, while psychological needs include emotional security, affection, and respect.

Many children with profound handicaps are unable to express, or even to identify, their own needs. Others may only be able to express them indirectly through whatever channel is available to them, and the care-taking adult must be alert and sensitive to each child's pattern of needs and method of communicating them. This is particularly true in toileting where the pattern of need varies so much between individuals. Appropriate attention to toileting needs has tremendous implications for children, both in influencing others' perceptions of them and in enhancing personal self-esteem. There can surely be few situations more undignified than being obliged to be incontinent because of lack of the necessary attention or assistance at the right time.

Other personal needs can be supplied in a more group-oriented and routine way. It is normal to have regular mealtimes, to wash, change clothes, work, and relax at certain times of the day, but these aspects of personal care must not become so routine that individual children's needs are ignored.

Although in providing care adults are primarily supplying children's deficit needs, caring can also contribute to their growth needs. Consistent management and handling in caring activities will allow children to understand and anticipate likely sequences of events. Even if they cannot participate actively in self-help tasks, they may learn to express their needs at appropriate times in a way which is generally understood, and so exercise some control over the pattern of care they receive. Many children can learn to cooperate and participate in some self-help activities. They may ultimately achieve a degree of independence and a resultant sense of achievement.

Factors which affect the care which children receive in school settings include:

CHILDREN'S PERSONAL CHARACTERISTICS

Children's personal characteristics will influence the pattern of care they experience. The amount of care will be determined by the form and severity of their handicap and the degree of assistance they require, as well as their personality and attractiveness to the care giver. Children who are responsive and rewarding to work with will almost inevitably be given more attention, even if this is quite unconscious on the part of the care-givers. Fortunately, different adults find different characteristics attractive; but some characteristics are almost universally appreciated whereas others are generally unappealing. Personal characteristics can affect the quality of care given and the relationship that develops between the care-givers and individual children.

CARE-GIVERS' PERSONAL QUALITIES

The personal qualities of the care-givers will also have a considerable effect on the care offered. Of particular importance are their degree of sensitivity to each child's needs and their ability to find ways of meeting them which preserve the children's dignity and allow self-determination. Another valuable quality is patience, which will allow children time for maximum exploitation of their learning potential and independence in self-help activities in an unhurried and pleasurable way.

Many parents of children with profound handicaps are, understandably, apprehensive when they start to attend school. Initially the parents' prime concern will be the quality of care given to the children in school. Well organised and sensitive personal care, which is part of a structured educational programme, will help parents to gain confidence in classroom staff, and to look beyond the deficit needs to the growth needs of their children.

THE TIME FACTOR

Practical considerations, such as the adult:child ratio, the arrangement of classroom facilities, and the organisation of routines associated with care-giving, will affect the amount of time available for caring activities. However, quantity and quality are not synonymous and must not be confused. If they are, the children's needs will not be met in the most beneficial way. An over-emphasis on caring activities can result in growth needs being unnecessarily subordinated to deficit needs. Less time devoted to the physical necessities will allow more time to be spent on the emotional and intellectual growth needs of the children through other aspects of the curriculum, and a careful balance must be maintained for each child.

Assessment and monitoring

It is the teacher's responsibility to plan children's programmes while they are at school. When considering individual aims for each of the children the teacher must take into account the children themselves as they are at the time, their potential abilities, and their future situation as far as it can be foreseen. Children's programmes must reflect the aims set for them as individuals and must make the best possible use of any facilities and support available in working towards them.

In order for the teacher to decide upon individual educational programmes the children's abilities must first be assessed and each one's major barriers to learning must be identified to ascertain an appropriate starting point. Formal assessment of children with profound handicaps is extremely difficult and the skills of all members of the classroom team, as well as the comments of the children's parents or care-givers, will be needed to produce a reasonably accurate profile of children's current abilities upon which to base a comprehensive educational programme. As far as possible an estimate of their potential abilities should be formed when the profiles are being compiled so that educational programmes can be devised which have appropriate priorities and realistic objectives for each individual.

Two aspects of the future must be considered: the children themselves, and their environment. By building upon children's physical, intellectual, and social abilities, and developing their range of skills, the educational programmes set will help children to become more effective in influencing their environment and controlling their experiences. Achievement, however slight, if it is valued by the staff will help to enable children to acquire a positive self-concept and increase their ability to derive satisfaction and benefit from any situation in which they may find themselves. Although their future situation cannot be definitely ascertained in advance, particularly in the present climate of change, some idea of the opportunities which are likely to be open may be known. The acquisition of self-help and independence skills, the ability to perform some tasks competently and reliably, however simple, may have a critical effect upon which opportunities will be offered to them when they finally leave school. The curriculum will also emphasise the acquisition of functional skills and knowledge which will be relevant in adulthood.

The skills of therapists and classroom assistants are not only necessary for the initial assessment of children's abilities and potential. They also contribute to the educational programme by working towards the same goals and sharing expertise and techniques with the teachers. All members of staff must be involved in monitoring children's progress and in planning and revising objectives so that each child's growth is a coordinated development rather than a fragmentary acquisition of unrelated skills.

All adults inevitably practise some degree of care when working with children with profound handicaps. The less obvious caring activities involved in forming relationships and offering emotional security and respect are practised in all their dealings with the children. These aspects of care are the foundations upon which the therapeutic and educational programmes will be built.

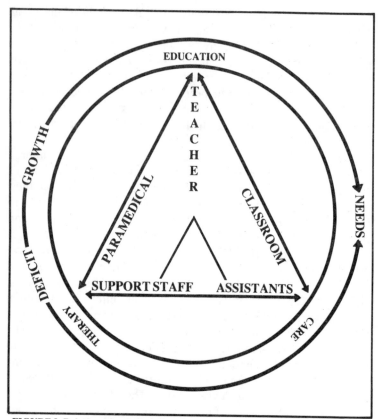

FIGURE 8. Relationship of education, therapy, and care in contributing to the needs of children with profound handicaps

The educational curriculum is the superstructure which, based on caring, considers children as "whole people", both at present and for the future, and offers educational programmes which encompass all areas of development and seek growth in all aspects. The therapeutic programmes provide extra support in some of the most important areas of development, and ensure the effectiveness of the whole programme. All are necessary. Without care children cannot survive; without enough care the best cannot be provided for them. Without therapy the effectiveness of educational programmes is reduced and children's disabilities have an unnecessarily great effect on their growth and development. Without education the child's experiences are not only impoverished but they are not balanced and coordinated and thus do not provide the basis for physical, mental, social, and emotional growth. Bruner (1960) has said:

> "the first object of any act of learning, over and beyond the pleasure it may give, is that it should serve us in the future. Learning should not only take us somewhere; it should allow us later to go further more easily".

How far children with profound handicaps can go depends upon all members of the classroom team working together towards the same goals (see Figure 8).

The notion of all members of the team regarding themselves as "developmental therapists", albeit with particular areas of expertise within that role, has much to recommend it in the classroom setting. It will help to overcome professional barriers between the different disciplines, and to ensure that an integrated approach is in operation at all times.

References

Bruner, J. S. *The Process of Education*. Harvard Univ. Press, 1960. Avail. from: London: American University Publishers Group.

Evans, P. L., Ware, J. *Special Care Provision: the education of children with profound and multiple learning difficulties*. Windsor: NFER/Nelson, 1987.

Hirst, P. The logic of the curriculum. *J. Curriculum Studies.*, 1969; **1**:2, 142-158.

Maslow, A. Deficiency motivation and growth motivation. *In* Jones, M. R. *Nebraska Symposium on Motivation*. Univ. Nebraska Press, 1955. Avail. from: London: American University Publishers Group.

Ouvry, C. *Considerations in Planning the Curriculum for the Profoundly Handicapped Child*. (Unpubl. thesis). London: Univ. London Institute of Education, 1983.

Schools Council Working Paper 70. *The Practical Curriculum*. London: Methuen Educational, 1981.

CHAPTER 7

A curriculum model

The concept of what constitutes an educational activity must be broadened greatly when considering the curriculum for children with profound handicaps. It can incorporate virtually any activity in virtually every situation in which such children are placed.

The curriculum has been defined as:

"the experiences each child has at school and what each child takes away" Schools Council Working Paper 70 (1981).

This includes not only the stated curriculum areas and the time-tabled activities which take place in the classroom, but also the hidden curriculum; that is, all those aspects which are an inherent part of any form of activity undertaken by children which give rise to feedback, often quite unconscious or at least unplanned, from adults and peers. Much of what would be part of the hidden curriculum in mainstream schools must be consciously defined and must form part of the stated curriculum in schools for children with severe learning difficulties; and this is even more true for children with profound handicaps. Activities which might be regarded as "care taking" are only confined to this role if the possibilities for using them as a learning situation are neglected.

Morgenstern (1981) stresses fragmentation of experience and learning as being a major obstacle to progress. This is particularly likely when children's experiences are not regarded as a continuous sequence of linked events by those who teach and care for them, and a different significance is attached to the activities which make up their day by various people in different roles. Every activity, whether primarily education, therapy, or care, incorporates elements of all three approaches. As school is first and foremost an educational establishment, the emphasis in the classroom must always be on the potential for learning that each activity offers.

Planning the curriculum

In discussion of the aims of education (Chapter 5) it was suggested that it is necessary to determine the overall aims for the group as a whole before any coherent curriculum planning can take place. It was stated that, firstly, these aims must be to consider children as members of society, taking into account characteristics which are desirable for children to develop as well as those which are unacceptable. Secondly, the aims must be to consider children as individuals and seek to promote in each one as great a degree of autonomy and self-determination as possible.

The curriculum, therefore, must provide a balance of activities which accommodate educational programmes which cover both aspects. This will involve two approaches: specific teaching programmes, and general experiences in a wider context, to cater for both depth and breadth of education.

Individual teaching programmes will have to be devised to help children to acquire skills that are appropriate to their individual capabilities and relevant to their present and probable future lifestyles, to eliminate or reduce behaviours which create barriers to learning or are socially unacceptable, and to minimise performance or management problems arising from their disabilities. These programmes will often be carried out in carefully structured, one-to-one or small group situations, but may take place in larger group activities which can also provide opportunities to work towards the specific objectives in children's individual programmes.

General experiences will need to be planned to compensate for the restrictions imposed by the children's disabilities, to help recognition and to promote understanding of their surroundings and the different situations that they encounter, and to offer opportunities for transfer of learning and generalisation of skills from specific learning situations to ordinary everyday activities. These experiences will be more freely structured, but will still be planned to form part of the coherent curriculum. They may take place in or outside school and involve one child or the whole group.

Cratty (1979) proposed a model containing four classifications of attributes — cognitive, perceptual, motor, and verbal — which develop at varying rates from the simple generalised ones present at birth to a proliferation of differentiated subattributes. These are bonded across the classifications to form complex modes of operation which can be compared with the sensori-motor schema described by Piaget (1953; 1954). Defects in any one classification will have adverse effects upon the development of skills and bonding processes in all classifications.

There is a considerable amount of published material available which gives detailed guidance on teaching children with profound handicaps specific skills (Simon, 1986; Kiernan, Jordan, and Saunders, 1978; Jeffrey, McConkey, and Hewson, 1977; Presland, 1982; to name but a few). More recently there have been some publications (Bailey, 1983; Browning *et al.*, 1983; Gardner, Murphy, and Crawford, 1983; Hogg and Sebba, 1986) which give guidance on planning an overall curriculum, which is vital if fragmentation of learning is to be avoided, the bonding processes promoted, and a coordinated programme carried out.

Without a basic structure to the curriculum there is a danger that the balance and coordination of activities for children with profound handicaps, which allow the bonding processes to take place, may be upset; or that the emphasis may revert to "caring" activities to the detriment of the children's all round progress.

Several authors have suggested areas which they regard as the "core" curriculum. Although these vary to some extent, the differences seem to be in labels and definitions rather than fundamentally different opinions as to the essential elements of the core curriculum (Gardner, Murphy, and Crawford, 1983; Gunstone, Hogg, Sebba, Warner, and Almond, 1982; Jeffrey, McConkey, and Hewson, 1977; Bailey, 1983).

The consensus as to the importance of certain core areas makes it possible to construct a curriculum model, which is likely to be generally appropriate for any class of children with profound handicaps, which will provide a unifying structure to guide the practical implementation of educational activities (see Figure 9). The model will need to be flexible so that the activities used can reflect the individual needs and capabilities of the children. It will also be influenced by factors such as the physical structure of the school, organisation of the school as a whole, and the resources available in terms of facilities, equipment, and staff in the special class. Having taken into consideration the constraints or opportunities presented by these factors the class teacher will select curriculum areas and devise activities which will contribute towards the progress of all the children in the class.

Developmental areas

When deciding which curriculum areas are appropriate for a group of children it is helpful first to consider four areas of development which should be catered for in each child's individual programme in order to ensure a balanced provision. These areas are physical, perceptual, intellectual, and personal/social

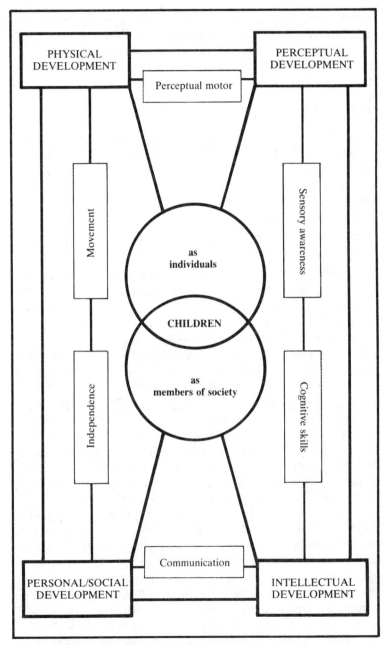

FIGURE 9. Curriculum model for children with profound handicaps

development. General aims can be identified for the children in each developmental area (see Appendix 2). These will form a link with the overall aims of education and will give some indication of the curriculum areas that are most likely to contribute towards the children's progress.

PHYSICAL DEVELOPMENT

Many children in special classes have some kind of physical impairment, frequently severe, so that there is an obvious and usually unambiguous need to promote motor development. It is through movement that children's response to the environment becomes overt and is made accessible to others. Karel Bobath (1980) points out that:

"a normal baby has a very wide range of behaviour with which
to express his needs, likes and dislikes other than crying".

Even children who have no apparent physical abnormality may have a very restricted and often stereotyped range of spontaneous movements which will limit their ability to interact with and learn from their surroundings.

In the area of motor development the general aims of the curriculum can be based on three different aspects — remedial, compensatory, and functional — which will all contribute towards the overall aim of increasing the range and control of self-initiated movements and thus enable the children to operate more effectively in their immediate surroundings. More specifically, the remedial aims will be: to prevent the development of abnormal patterns of movement and to counteract deformities or dysfunction resulting from the children's impairments; and to promote normal patterns of physical development, thus enabling the children to participate more fully in activities requiring voluntary movement. The compensatory aims will be: to provide children with movement experiences, whether active or passive, which would otherwise be denied them in order to encourage enjoyment of physical activity and development of confidence in movement; to promote perception of movement and postural awareness; and to increase self-awareness and allow children to construct a realistic body image and sense of personal space. The functional aims will be: to seek to promote active, goal directed movement which increases the children's ability to control and shape their own movements; to increase differentiation of fine movements and improve manipulative skills; and to increase mobility and locomotive skills.

Progress towards these aims will enable children to participate in activities in all the curriculum areas, thus reducing the risk of fragmentation of experience, and allow them to exercise some degree of control over their own environment and experience.

PERCEPTUAL DEVELOPMENT

Many children with profound handicaps have at least one sensory impairment. The resultant uneven and restricted sensory development presents them with a major barrier to learning. Perceptual development includes all the senses; vision, hearing, touch, taste, smell, and proprioception. Children with profound handicaps are often referred to as "understimulated" because of their commonly low level of spontaneous activity. The remedy is assumed to be "to stimulate them", but people rarely ask "stimulate them to do what?".

The notion that any reflex or random response to stimulation is better than nothing is debatable. Exposing children to a kaleidoscope of unrelated events may only add to their existing confusion, either because the input is distorted or because they cannot select or extract meaning from the information. This may result in them showing an increase in disorganised behaviour, or a withdrawal as they attempt to reduce the anxiety and confusion caused.

Even if it has not been identified, the possibility of sensory impairment must always be considered and efforts made to establish whether it exists and the extent of the impairment. It is extremely important, whether sensory impairment is present or not, to have a clear idea of the aims in the area of perceptual development before embarking on a course of sensory "stimulation".

Various aspects must be considered when identifying the general aims of perceptual development. Firstly, children must be encouraged to use all their senses, including those in which there may be some degree of deficit, in order to improve their efficiency in acquiring information from the environment. Secondly, they must be encouraged to compensate for deficits in one area by increasing the range and sensitivity of perception in other areas, and integrating the sensory information gained.

The overall aim will be to develop children's perceptual abilities to the fullest possible extent, so that they can derive and use the maximum amount of information from their surroundings. Additional aims will be: to promote children's awareness of self in relation to their environment and help them to establish consistent response to change; to encourage children to direct their attention towards the source of stimulation and to teach them to become more selective about attention-giving in order to facilitate the development of discrimination; to increase children's acuity, thus improving their ability to discriminate between stimuli in the same modality; and to encourage their awareness of the various properties of different stimuli so that they can form concepts related to vision, sound, touch, taste, smell, and movement.

Although development of all the senses will be covered in the curriculum, the dominant ones of vision and hearing are likely to have priority in the timetable because of their importance in facilitating learning in all the curriculum areas.

INTELLECTUAL DEVELOPMENT

Intellectual development is a product of children's experiences and the cognitive processes which they use to extrapolate meaning from those experiences and so understand their environment. Children who are profoundly handicapped are detrimentally affected in both aspects. The nature of their disabilities inevitably restricts access to many situations and events which are day-to-day experiences for other children. They have few strategies for exploring their surroundings and so are deprived of opportunities to test their hypotheses about the nature of their environment. This prevents them from appreciating the significance of events and constructing a realistic model of the world.

The overall aims of intellectual development will be to compensate for children's restriction and fragmentation of experience, and to encourage the development of cognitive processes which will enable them to integrate their experiences and will aid their understanding of the surroundings and the society in which they live. More specifically, the aims will be: to promote children's progress through the early global patterns of response, from reflex or coincidental responses to intentional and goal-directed actions; to encourage adult-child interactions and the focusing of mutual attention on an external stimulus or referent; to establish a systematic means of communication with individual children to allow effective teaching situations to be set up; to promote children's formation of concepts through selection and integration of sensory information; to promote children's use of effective learning strategies and a repertoire of actions which will enable them to explore and control their surroundings; to establish in children the ability to make considered choices and appropriate decisions in a variety of situations; and to extend children's competence in a range of tasks so that they can occupy themselves appropriately.

PERSONAL/SOCIAL DEVELOPMENT

This is a very broad area, concerned with children as individuals and as members of society. It encompasses those skills and characteristics which will enable children to become accepted participants in social situations and which will encourage their emotional development. Positive self-concept and self-esteem depends partly upon children's ability to operate effectively and to take responsibility for themselves, and partly upon the value placed upon their achievements by others. The ability of all members of the classroom team to see and appreciate the efforts and achievements of children with profound handicaps is essential for the personal and emotional well-being of the children, whose level of independence and ability to control their surroundings is so limited.

The overall aim in this area will be to enable children to develop a positive self-concept, and the skills and confidence necessary to become a participating member of society. More specific aims will be: to enable children to tolerate, cooperate, and participate in activities, and to become an acceptable member of a group; to encourage children's awareness of their own personal needs and preferences and their ability to make decisions and take responsibility for these; to enable children to achieve the maximum possible independence in personal care compatible with their disabilities; to encourage children to interact with others so that they can enjoy being part of a group and can join in activities that involve sharing, turn-taking, and cooperating with others; and to establish appropriate channels of communication which will enable them to express their own personalities and take an active part in social situations.

Many of these aims may seem unattainable for children who are profoundly handicapped, but with carefully structured teaching programmes and the greatest possible degree of opportunity they can achieve some measure of progress. Denying children even the

Developmental areas	Core curriculum	Components
PHYSICAL	Movement	Gross motor Body image Physiotherapy
	Perceptual motor	Fine motor Occupation skills
PERCEPTUAL	Sensory awareness	Vision Hearing Touch Taste/Smell Proprioception
INTELLECTUAL	Cognitive skills	Basic skills Concept formation Situational understanding
	Communication	Interaction patterns Cognitive processes Receptive ⎱ Expressive ⎰ communication
PERSONAL/SOCIAL	Independence	Self-help/Daily living Environmental control

FIGURE 10. Suggested curriculum structure for children with profound handicaps

slightest chance to exercise independence reduces their dignity and sense of worth, and allowing them to do so demands considerable restraint on the part of the adults involved. Encouraging and allowing time for children to use self-help or independence skills, or to join in reciprocal social interactions, and creating situations where they can practise communication skills, requires careful planning, patience, and sensitivity on the part of every adult whether in the special class or the main school.

The core curriculum

The four developmental areas that have just been described are very broad, but they give some indication of the more specific core curriculum which might contribute towards children's progress in all aspects of development. Each core area has several components which together can provide the range of activities necessary to cater for the diverse needs of the children (see Figure 10).

A wide range of activities is carried out in schools for children with severe learning difficulties, but in a survey of 12 schools (Ouvry, 1983) it emerged that certain areas are central to every school curriculum for the special class. Each school visited included movement, self-help or independence skills, communication, and perception in its timetable. A few schools mentioned a range of other activities but most of these would form components of the core curriculum, or would fall into the category of activities designed to widen pupils' general experiences. With the addition of various forms of creative activities these areas are generally confirmed in the survey based on 65 classes in schools in the South East of England (Evans and Ware, 1987).

Figure 9 (page 95) illustrates one useful curriculum model. The developmental areas are shown in relation to the core curriculum areas, each of which contributes to all the developmental areas to a greater or lesser extent. Although some of the terms and the format of the model may differ, these curriculum areas correspond quite closely to those suggested by Gunstone, Hogg, Sebba, Warner, and Almond (1982) and Bailey (1983) specifically for teaching children with profound handicaps.

The core curriculum is made up of six areas — movement, perceptual motor skills, sensory awareness, cognitive skills, communication, and independence skills. Each core area comprises several component areas which provide the flexibility that is necessary when catering for such a heterogeneous group of children. A more detailed discussion of each core area and its components follows in Chapter 8.

Once the core curriculum and the components have been defined, general aims and objectives can be stated within each area. This is frequently done by referring to a checklist based on normal development (Dale, 1977; Bluma, Shearer, Frohman, and Hilliard, 1976) from which objectives can be selected for individual children for any given activity. This has the advantage of providing a firm structure which incorporates a form of assessment, but the disadvantage that the content may be irrelevant to the pattern of development of children who are profoundly handicapped.

Kiernan (1981) warns that the pattern of progress of such children may not be directly along the route of normal development; and too strict an adharence to normal developmental sequences can be counterproductive in the context of a functional curriculum for them. A skills model, which may be expressed in the form of behavioural objectives but which follows a developmental sequence where appropriate, is generally more useful, both for monitoring progress and for suggesting the next stage of teaching.

Published material on specific teaching programmes is available (Simon, 1986; Kiernan, Jordan, and Saunders, 1978; Kiernan, 1981; Cooper, Moodley, and Reynell, 1978). Although they do not cover a comprehensive curriculum they are extremely useful as a basis for core curriculum areas and can help teachers compile a list of objectives suitable for their particular groups of children.

Expressive objectives, which are not stated in behavioural terms but which define the experiences that are to be offered to children rather than the precise responses the activities are designed to elicit, are also very important. This is particularly true when activities are designed to compensate for experiences which have been denied them as a result of their disabilities, or when they are intended to increase children's appreciation and understanding of themselves and their environment. Experience, of speed and momentum in movement activities, of different tastes or varying textures and surfaces in sensory awareness, or of tension and release in a drama session, cannot be defined in behavioural terms; but it is essential if the curriculum is to be more than a succession of skills training sessions. Music, art, drama, play, and many other activities which contribute to the extended curriculum, are compatible with the expressive approach.

The curriculum areas are identified with "the whole child" in mind. This includes children's physical, mental, and affective state; their unique characteristics and needs as individuals; and the standards of behaviour demanded of them as members of society. Although many children with profound handicaps can progress only a very short way towards the ultimate goals of autonomy and self-determination, careful identification of aims and analysis of interim stages will ensure that progress, whether great or small, can be made and noted.

Planning individual programmes

Once the curriculum structure and its broad content has been defined, programmes for individual children can be devised by referring to the successive levels within the curriculum structure and selecting those parts which are appropriate for each one. The relationship between the general curriculum and individual programmes is shown in Figure 11 (see page 104). No individual curriculum profile will include all the aims of the general curriculum, and it is unlikely that every curriculum component will be represented in any one child's individual programme.

Children's programmes must be carefully planned, using selected curriculum components, to form a coherent and balanced programme of activities. The emphasis will depend upon the children's existing abilities and the handicaps and obstructions to learning that result from their disabilities. The aim is to enable the children to acquire functional skills which will be of practical use and which will compensate to some extent for their disabilities. Programmes must also attempt to fill the gaps in the children's experience, so that their understanding is increased and their skills can be generalised and used appropriately in a variety of situations.

Consultation with parents and care givers is extremely important at this stage and their wishes must be reflected in the children's programmes. A survey carried out for Mencap (Hogg, Lambe, Cowie, and Coxon, 1987) indicated that there were several main areas of general concern to parents in terms of their children's development, namely: language and communication, gross and fine motor development, dealing with behaviour problems, and the ability to enjoy leisure activities. All of these areas should be incorporated in a comprehensive teaching programme at a level appropriate for each individual child.

If parents and caregivers are involved in the planning of programmes, this will ensure that skills are taught which are

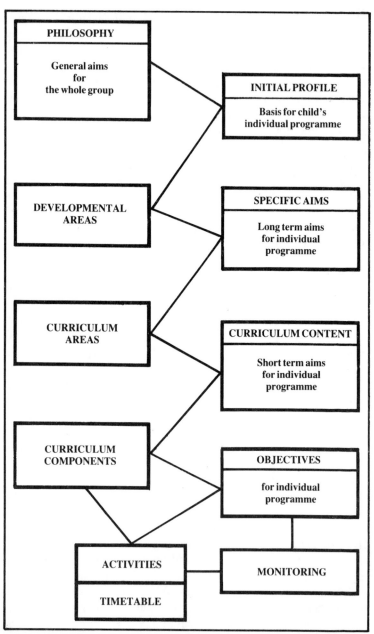

FIGURE 11. The importance of curriculum structure in individual programme
planning

considered to be most essential in *all* aspects of the children's lives. The relevance to their life at home of skills taught at school will be more fully appreciated, and this will make it much more likely that work done at school will be reinforced and consolidated when the children are at home.

It is essential, before identifying aims, selecting curriculum areas, or devising activities, to carry out a preliminary assessment in order to produce a profile of each child's mode of functioning, attempt to predict future progress, indicate areas of priority for teaching, and provide a baseline from which to plan their individual programmes and to monitor their progress.

Assessment and programming

Assessment has been defined as:

"gaining knowledge about the behaviour, abilities and attitudes of the child in order to select appropriate objectives. It defines the entry point for a child into the curriculum" (Leeming, Swann, Coupe, and Mittler, 1979).

Standardised assessment checklists, with pass/fail criteria, which are designed to be completed in a single session will certainly fail to produce a reliable picture of any child's functioning, especially if the child is profoundly handicapped.

In the survey by Evans and Ware (1986) more than half the children were reported to be untested by psychological assessment procedures, and 19 different tests were mentioned. The 12-school survey (Ouvry, 1983) showed that although various checklists were used none was found to be particularly satisfactory. Assessments which are very detailed have two disadvantages: they take too long for class teachers to complete and the major findings may be obscured by the welter of information they collect. On the other hand assessments can be oversimplified and so fail to give adequate information on some of the most crucial features for teaching. Many assessments take the form of developmental checklists based on normal development with the disadvantages already discussed above. Others have been specially constructed for assessing one specific area of development. Appendix 3 lists some assessments and checklists which are, or purport to be, relevant for children operating at a very early developmental level.

Kiernan (1976) has suggested four steps that can be taken to establish a basis for deciding on urgent priorities in teaching.

Firstly, developmental blocks, such as behaviour problems, or sensory or physical deficits, should be identified. These are the obstructions to learning which individual programmes will seek to eliminate or by-pass so that teaching can be effective. Secondly, children's needs and preferences should be identified for use as rewards during teaching. These may be food or drink, some kind of sensory stimulation such as vibration or lights, or social contact and praise. It may be necessary with some children to provide a wide range of sensory experiences before any identification of preferences is possible. Thirdly, children's levels of socialisation and communication must be assessed. Until some form of interaction between children and adult has been established children will be unable to respond to the adult's demand for action. Finally, children's spontaneous activity and sensori-motor coordination must be evaluated. Here it is important to note the level of activity, whether actions are random or purposeful, and what motivates the activity. This will show whether children have the exploratory skills necessary to find out about their environment spontaneously, or whether their individual programmes must include training or practice in these basic skills before more complex learning can be introduced. It is also important to identify children's achievements in independence skills, noting whether these are on the level of exercising self-help skills and participating in personal care, or whether they are confined to indicating need or discomfort, by whatever means available to them, and accepting the attention of caregivers.

Leeming, Swann, Coupe, and Mittler (1979) suggest that observation falls into three broad categories: general observation from a distance, of children's interaction with the environment; specific observation of finer details of children's behaviour; and intervention/observation when children's response to an adult's intervention is noted. Careful distance observation of children during day-to-day classroom activities should produce a reasonably comprehensive initial profile. Any gaps can be filled by sessions designed to assess detailed aspects of their performance, with or without intervention.

Appendix 1 suggests a suitable format for an Initial Profile which seeks to ensure that no major aspects are overlooked and aims to facilitate the planning of individual programmes based on the curriculum model that has been described. It consists of four sections, which correspond to the four developmental areas of the curriculum and cover the four questions posed by Kiernan (1976). It is not in the form of a checklist, since many of the items would inevitably be irrelevant for many children with profound handicaps but subheadings in each area suggest the most important points to be observed. The resulting record will describe the way each child operates and the major barriers to learning in each developmental area. This information is most important as it is often necessary to eliminate, or at least reduce, these obstructions before a reasonable estimate can be made of the level at which teaching should take place.

The Initial Profile will show where more detailed, in-depth assessment is needed before programme planning can take place. For this teachers may use one of the more detailed general assessments available which cover all areas, such as the *Behaviour Assessment Battery* (Kiernan and Jones, 1977), the *Anson House Checklist* (Hester Adrian Research Centre, 1979), the *NSL Developmental Assessment Scale* (Simon, 1981), the *Callier Azusa Scale* (Stillman, 1986), or the *Progress Guide for Deaf/Blind and/or Severely Handicapped Children* (Dale, 1977). Alternatively they may choose an assessment which concentrates on a particular area, such as the *Paths to Mobility Checklist* (Presland, 1982), *Preverbal Communication Schedule* (Kiernan and Reid, 1986) *Feeding Checklist* (Warner, 1981), or *Object Related Scheme Assessment Procedure* (Coupe and Levy, 1985). Where specialist support is available, such as peripatetic teachers of children with visual or hearing impairments, or medical or paramedical services, such as the orthoptist or audiologist, speech therapist, and physio-therapist, the appropriate professionals can be asked to provide in-depth assessments of children's needs and abilities in their specialist areas and to advise on suitable teaching programmes and methods.

Many children with profound handicaps have very little voluntary control of their movements or have strong residual reflexes. They may be constantly moving in an uncoordinated and apparently random way, or they may be extremely passive and inert. In either case it will be very difficult to gain an accurate idea of their child's conscious responses to their surroundings from general observation. They may appear to be unresponsive or uncomprehending if their responses are masked by an inability to produce consistent voluntary movements. More detailed observations will then have to be carried out, sometimes over a long period of time, before a baseline for teaching can be decided. Frequently it is necessary to record every response to a range of stimuli presented within a structured situation before any consistent pattern can be detected. Videotape recordings of such sessions can be helpful in that no details are missed, and they can be viewed repeatedly or compared with recordings of subsequent sessions.

The completed Initial Profiles will identify the priority areas for teaching. General aims for the children's individual programmes can then be selected from the General Aims of Education (Appendix 2) within each developmental area. If these aims are not appropriate for any of the children they can be amended, or further aims can be added to produce a comprehensive list of appropriate long-term aims for each individual. The priority for every child is likely to be either in the area in which their greatest deficit lies, or the area which shows the greatest potential for progress. It is very important, however, to set aims in each of the four developmental areas to ensure a balanced programme and to avoid fragmentation of experience.

The curriculum areas and the components which are most relevant and most likely to contribute towards achieving the aims set for the children can now be selected, and short-term aims identified within each curriculum area. Again, these can be taken from the aims already identified for the curriculum area or, if necessary, new aims can be identified.

The teaching objectives for the individual programmes can now be stated. Reference to the objectives identified for the curriculum components included in the programmes may suggest relevant teaching objectives at appropriate levels for individual children. If not, new objectives can be included. The conditions and criteria for success should be set out in detail for every objective. Activities to promote their achievement will have to be devised. Some of these will be implicit in the conditions stated for the objectives but, particularly in the case of expressive objectives, this will not always be the case.

The activities devised may be one-to-one, intensive teaching involving stringent behavioural objectives, such as attention training, development of listening skills, or use of electronic aids; or they may involve group work in which more flexible, individual objectives for each child are incorporated into the activities of the group as a whole, such as during movement sessions, meal times, drama sessions, or times when they are using free play materials.

There are several sources of ideas for teaching available, such as the audio-visual aids, and equipment to make or buy, listed in Appendix 4. Other information can be found in books and periodicals, some of which are listed with the relevant areas of the curriculum described in the next chapter. Whichever activities are selected or devised, they must suit the objectives set for the children and must form a coherent framework of experience for individual children, with opportunities to practise and generalise the skills acquired in intensive learning sessions. This requires much insight and ingenuity on the part of teachers responsible for planning and implementing the programmes.

As the profile of each child's functioning is unique, so the curriculum profile and the specific teaching programmes will vary considerably between individual children. Chapter 8 discusses each curriculum area and its components in greater detail and suggests some activities which can be used to work towards the objectives set in individual programmes.

References

Anson House Checklists. (Anson House Pre-school Project). Manchester: Hester Adrian Research Centre, 1979.

Bailey, I. J. *Structuring a Curriculum for Profoundly Mentally Handicapped Children.* Glasgow: Jordanhill College of Education, 1983.

Bluma, S., Shearer, M., Frohman, A., Hilliard, J. *Portage Guide to Early Education.* Windsor: NFER-Nelson, 1976.

Bobath, K. *A Neurophysiological Basis for the Treatment of Cerebral Palsy.* London: SIMP, 1980.

Browning, M. M., Anderson, C. A., Bailey, I. J., Law, I. H., MacLeod, C., Suckling, M. M. *Identifying the Needs of Profoundly Mentally Handicapped Children.* Glasgow: Jordanhill College of Education, 1983.

Cooper, J., Moodley, M., Reynell, J. *Helping Language Development.* London: Edward Arnold, 1978.

Coupe, J., Levy, D. The object related scheme assessment procedure. *Ment. Hand.,* 1985; **13**:2, 22-24.

Cratty, B. J. *Perceptual and Motor Development in Infants and Children.* Hemel Hempstead: Prentice-Hall Inc., 1979.

Dale, F. J. *Progress Guide for Deaf/Blind and/or Severely Handicapped Children.* (2nd edn.). London: National Deaf-Blind and Rubella Assoc., 1977.

Evans, P. L., Ware, J. *Special Care Provision: The Education of Children with Profound and Multiple Learning Difficulties.* Windsor: NFER/Nelson, 1987.

Gardner, J., Murphy, J., Crawford, N. *The Skills Analysis Model.* Kidderminster: BIMH Publications, 1983.

Gunstone, C., Hogg, J., Sebba, J., Warner, J., Almond, S. *Classroom Provision and Organisation for Integrated Pre-school Children.* Barkingside: Barnardo's, 1982.

Hogg, J., Lambe, L., Cowie, J., Coxon, J. *People with Profound Retardation and Multiple Handicaps Attending Schools or Social Education Centres.* London: Mencap, 1987.

Hogg, J., Sebba, J. *Profound Retardation and Multiple Impairment (Vols. 1 and 2).* London: Croom Helm, 1986.

Jeffrey, D., McConkey, R., Hewson, S. *Teaching the Handicapped Child.* London: Souvenir Press, 1977.

Kiernan, C. *Analysis of Programmes for Teachers.* Basingstoke: Globe Educational, 1981.

Kiernan, C., Jones, M. C. *Behaviour Assessment Battery.* Windsor: NFER/Nelson, 1977.

Kiernan, C., Jordan, R., Saunders, C. *Starting Off.* London: Souvenir Press, 1978.

Kiernan, C., Reid, B. *Pre-Verbal Communication Schedule.* Windsor: NFER/Nelson, 1986.

Kiernan, C. *Towards a Curriculum for the Profoundly Handicapped Child.* (Report of a Conference held at Northern Counties College on September 14-16, 1976). Newcastle: Petras Div. Newcastle-upon-Tyne Poly., 1976.

Leeming, K., Swann, W., Coupe, J., Mittler, P. *Teaching Language and Communication to the Mentally Handicapped.* (Schools Council Curriculum Bulletin 8). London: Evans/Methuen Educational, 1979.

Morgenstern, F. *Teaching Plans for Handicapped Children.* London: Methuen, 1981.

Ouvry, C. *Considerations in Planning the Curriculum for the Profoundly Handicapped.* (Unpubl. thesis). London: Univ. London Inst. of Education, 1983.

Piaget, J. *Construction of Reality in the Child.* (Trans. Cook, M.). London: Routledge and Kegan Paul, 1954.

Piaget, J. *The Origin of Intelligence in the Child.* (Trans. Cook, M.). London: Routledge and Kegan Paul, 1953.

Presland, J. L. *Paths to Mobility in "Special Care".* Kidderminster: BIMH Publications, 1982.

Presland, J. L. *The Paths to Mobility Checklist — objectives for teaching gross motor skills to "special care" children.* Kidderminster: BIMH Publications, 1982.

Schools Council Working Paper 70: The Practical Curriculum. London: Evans/Methuen Educational, 1981.

Simon, G. B. *The Next Step on the Ladder: assessment and management of children with multiple handicaps. (4th Edn.).* Kidderminster: BIMH Publications, 1986.

Simon, G. B. *The NSL Developmental Assessment Scale — summary, personal record, and progress review charts.* Kidderminster: BIMH Publications, 1981.

Stillman, R. (Ed.). *The Callier-Azusa Scale.* Dallas: University of Texas at Dallas, Callier Center for Communication Disorders, 1986.

Warner, J. *Helping the Handicapped Child with Early Feeding.* Winslow: Winslow Press, 1981.

CHAPTER 8

The core curriculum

Considerably more attention has, in recent years, been turned towards the content of the curriculum for children with profound handicaps. General stimulation is no longer considered to be sufficient, or even desirable. The 12-school survey (Ouvry, 1983) found, however, that few special classes had a general curriculum statement for the class as a whole, and frequently there was no distinction between the curriculum and the timetable. It seemed that, because of lack of reference material, teachers adopted their own personal approach and, of necessity, devised the activities used to carry out teaching programmes. The number of activities and the many different names used to identify core curriculum areas reflects this wide variation in approach.

It is impossible to separate one curriculum area from another since they all overlap and each contributes, to a greater or lesser extent, to all four developmental areas. It is necessary, however, for the purpose of curriculum planning and implementation, to refer to a curriculum structure in which the main areas and components are distinguished to ensure that a balanced and comprehensive curriculum is offered which is relevant to the needs of individual children and to the group as a whole. The curriculum model described in the preceding chapter has been found most useful in providing a unifying structure which allows for continuity and development, both of which are so vital in teaching children with profound handicaps. It also ensures that the adverse consequences of staff changeover are kept to a minimum. A discussion of the six core areas, and suggestions for activities which might be used when working in them, follows.

Movement

The 12-school survey (Ouvry, 1983) showed that a large number of children in special classes have a physical impairment in addition to their mental handicap. Consequently, the motor area of the curriculum is considered a priority in all schools. Research into the role of movement in perceptual and intellectual development has produced conflicting opinions (Kephart, 1960; Held and Hein,

1963; Bruner, 1968; Bower, 1977). It is indisputable, however, that any limitation or abnormality in children's movement patterns will inevitably affect their interaction with the surroundings and their power to influence their environment and exert control over their experiences, either directly or indirectly. The effect of specific physical disabilities will be compounded if the children are also mentally handicapped and the problems they face in organising and influencing their experiences in all areas will be increased.

There are some children who have no physical limitation of movement but who nevertheless use a very restricted range of spontaneous movements. These restricted movements limit their awareness of their own personal space and the relationship of their own body to objects in their immediate surroundings. They often have poor muscle tone and a low level of activity which affects the frequency and nature of their actions and the experiences and opportunities for learning which arise out of them.

Whatever the underlying cause, difficulties in initiating and performing effective actions which allow exploration or change of their surroundings inhibits children's efforts to interact with their environment. They become more dependent upon others to provide experiences in movement, and indeed all other areas, to compensate for experiences they cannot gain for themselves.

Bruner (1968) has postulated that voluntary control of movement involves anticipation and outcome, selecting the means to achieve a goal, the ability to sustain behaviour, and the ability to mobilise an intended response. Voluntary movement is a highly complex skill which requires: sensory input in the form of auditory, visual, tactile, and kinaesthetic stimuli; mediating processes, such as attention, selection, analysis, and interpretation, which transform input into organised perceptions and select the goal for output; and the output itself, which involves intention and the forming and execution of a motor plan to produce the desired movement. It depends upon delicately balanced patterns of muscular activity which may lead to an observable change of position of any part of the body or may alternatively result in the maintenance of the body in a stable position, as when resisting a force or using the postural mechanisms to provide a stable base from which active movements can take place.

The movement curriculum should take into consideration at which of these stages motor control can be influenced and also the implications of dysfunction in any of these stages for the production of movement. It should include activities aimed not only at performance but also at elicitation and organisation of movement. For children who have very little voluntary movement it may be possible to build up a range of movement experiences by activating the mediating processes, even if the output must be in the form of passive movements.

There is a very close correspondence between the movement curriculum area and the broad area of physical development discussed in Chapter 7. The general aims will be essentially the same, but in the curriculum will be elaborated within the component areas. In this curriculum model the component areas cover physiotherapy, gross motor skills, and body image.

THE PHYSIOTHERAPY COMPONENT

This component contributes the remedial and preventive aspects of the movement curriculum and provides much of the individual movement programme for children who need it. The aims will be:

to prevent abnormal posture and patterns of movement from developing;

to remedy or reduce deformities or dysfunction resulting from disabilities;

to encourage normal patterns of physical development and functional patterns of action.

Physiotherapy programmes will be highly specific to individual children. Physiotherapists will be responsible for defining objectives and devising exercises for their individual programmes. They can also give guidance to other members of staff about positioning and types of movement which will be beneficial to children in various situations and activities, and which will help indirectly, to achieve the stated aims. The amount of time physiotherapists spend in school affects the balance between the advisory and treatment aspects of their role, and the extent to which their expertise is confined to individual remedial programmes or is extended to support the movement curriculum for all the pupils.

THE GROSS MOTOR COMPONENT

This component incorporates compensatory and functional movement activities. The wide variation of motor abilities of children in a special class, ranging from normal physical development to almost total absence of voluntary movement, results in a correspondingly large number of aims, including:

to increase confidence in movement and enjoyment of physical activity;

to compensate for restricted movement experiences through active/passive participation in various movement activities;

to extend the range and control of movements initiated;

to promote motor organisation and the ability to carry out purposeful movements;

to improve balance and postural mechanisms and encourage mobility and locomotor skills;

to increase agility, strength, and coordination.

There are many different movement activities which provide a variety of experiences and possibilities for learning:

Developmental movement, in which the adult works in close physical contact with the children, is closely attuned to their responses, and can thus promote confidence and enjoyment of movement, at the same time encouraging coordinated whole body movements and a range and quality of movements not otherwise experienced by the children;

Music and movement, in which the music helps to initiate spontaneous movement and imposes rhythm and pattern on the movement sequences, thereby facilitating organisation of movements;

Drama games, in which rhymes and songs cue the movement experiences, thereby encouraging anticipation and active participation;

Swimming, which can induce a degree of relaxation and freedom of movement not easily achieved by other means;

Apparatus, including climbing frames, slides, steps, balance boards, benches, and inflatables, all of which can be used to promote specific movements and generally improve balance, coordination, agility, and strength.

Mobility, in which children are encouraged to move from place to place and explore the surroundings confidently, the emphasis being either upon independence, in which case the most effective means of locomotion — crawling, walking with or without aids, or using a wheelchair — will be practised, or upon encouraging more normal forms of locomotion through progress from earlier forms to independent walking.

Although ideally the activities will encourage active, self-initiated and directed movement, passive movement will be necessary for children with limited voluntary control and a restricted range of movements. This will provide them with experiences which are usually denied to them and will encourage interpersonal interaction through shared movement experiences.

Movement activities will overlap with the other developmental areas: sensory development can be promoted by linking movements with vision, hearing, and touch so that children can perceive, anticipate, and participate in patterns of movement; and cognitive development can be promoted by interaction with the environment through controlled and purposeful movements and understanding of concepts related to movement, such as position and direction and the temporal and spatial aspects.

THE BODY IMAGE COMPONENT

This component contributes towards children's perception of their own bodies and movements. Body image is a very variable concept, but Cratty (1979) suggests that it includes "the responses the child makes relative to his or her body's shape, size, components, perceived capacity for movement and interactions with the environment".

Children with very restricted movements, whether because of physical disability or inactivity, will have limited experience of the range of movements possible and of their own personal space, largely because of the constant invasion of personal space which they undergo as others carry out their personal care.

Sherborne (1979) stresses the importance of developing awareness of the body as a whole and the body centre as the basis for controlled and coordinated movements of the limbs and the formation of concepts of laterality and directionality. A realistic body image and sense of personal space is most important in the organisation of functional movements in relation to people, objects, and the immediate environment. Thus, the aims are:

to encourage body symmetry and midline orientation;

to promote use of the full range of movements and awareness

of personal space;

to promote accurate adjustment of movements and body position in relation to the surroundings or task;

to encourage the ability to imitate gross and fine actions;

to establish the ability to identify body parts;

to establish the ability to follow instructions in relation to position or direction of movement;

to promote the safe negotiation of obstacles and reach the intended destination.

All activities which involve movement will contain an element of body concept work, but in some it can be particularly emphasised:

Developmental movement, already described above, in which the positions and movements introduced can encourage children to differentiate between their own movements and the adult's movement and to appreciate the relationship of their body both to the adult and to their physical surroundings;

Swimming, in which the sensation of the water and the result of movements enhances children's awareness of the position of their body and limbs;

Riding, in which children's awareness of body position is enhanced by the smell, tactile sensations, and movements of the horse;

Music and movement, such as music therapy and other activity programmes, in which music is used to initiate and guide patterns of movement involving different parts of the body;

Directed movement, in which precise movements can be initiated and controlled by the use of language in the form of chants, rhymes, and songs;

Massage, in which parts of the body — arms and hands, legs and feet, shoulders or back — are massaged with textures and substances, such as velvet or towelling, talcum powder or oil, to heighten awareness of them and induce general relaxation;

Mirror work, in which children's attention to their own movements is attracted by the reflections in the mirror;

Small apparatus, particularly things which produce different sensations such as vibration (beach balls, vibrators), air flow (squeezy bottles, blankets), or weight and resistance (bean bags), which can help to focus children's attention on various body parts and emphasise body symmetry and midline, the large

joints, and the relative position of limbs and trunk;
Large apparatus, described in the gross motor section, which can
also be used to enhance children's perception of their position
and movements in relation to the physical environment.

Planning and implementing the movement curriculum will
involve the close cooperation of all members of the interdisciplinary
classroom team. The role of the physiotherapist will be particularly
important, but it is the responsibility of the teacher to ensure that
remedial, compensatory, and functional aspects are incorporated
into a curriculum which avoids fragmentation of experience and
allows children's needs to be catered for in a coherent movement
programme.

Sensory awareness

Sensory perception provides the information upon which
children base their understanding of the surroundings and which
guides their responses to the environment. It depends upon
children's awareness of the sensory stimuli around them and their
ability to select and integrate those which are salient, making
meaningful associations and assimilating them with previous
experience. It is impossible, in practice, to separate the perceptual
and cognitive processes; but it is important to include a curriculum
area in which the emphasis is on input rather than mental
processing, and in which carefully structured activities are used to
encourage children to use all the channels available to them to gain
information about the environment.

It is generally acknowledged that there is a basic need for sensory
stimulation but that there is a limit to the amount of information
that can be processed. Children with profound handicaps including
severe sensory deficits may be unable to acquire a satisfactory level
of stimulation from their surroundings, or they may be confused
and overwhelmed by the impressions they receive and their inability
to filter and organise the information. They may develop bizarre,
stereotyped, or self-injurious behaviours, or light play to provide
sensations which are under their control. Unfortunately these
inhibit the abilities they do possess and effectively reduce even
further their interaction with the environment and the information
they gain from it.

In the 12-school survey (Ouvry, 1983) one third of the children in
special classes were reported to have severe impairment of one or

more senses. The number of children with some degree of sensory loss may be even higher, since it is very difficult to identify deficits with any degree of certainty in children with profound handicaps. Where there is impairment of more than one sense, particularly the dominant senses of vision and hearing, children's difficulties are greatly compounded and their access to information enormously reduced and distorted. Any deficit or distortion will significantly affect their awareness of the relationship between themselves and their environment, and thus their ability to organise and control their experiences.

Sensory perception is an integral part of every activity and, however severely handicapped people may be, some kind of experience is bound to occur through one of the senses. The minimal or inconsistent responses elicited, however, may make it extremely difficult to detect any reliable indication of sensory awareness. Without a consistent pattern of response to sensory stimuli in any given channel, neither perception nor lack of perception can be assumed. It may be necessary to teach a response, before introducing a range of stimuli in any modality, in order to help to establish a response threshold in any one sensory area.

If children are to be able to use information from their surroundings, the sensory component and its meaning for them (insofar as this can be estimated) must be taken into account. Activities must be structured and presented in a way that will increase their awareness of the salient features and facilitate the organisation and integration of the information provided. Bower (1977) stresses the importance of sensory inputs which are appropriate to children's abilities. Bombardment of children with multi-sensory stimuli will only create confusion and inhibit learning. It will do nothing to help them select, discriminate, and interpret the information. It is necessary instead to reduce the amount of information presented and to enhance and simplify the characteristics of the materials used so that they are readily perceived and their properties are understood by the children. Particular care must be given to the selection of activities, materials and equipment, and methods of presentation. Children must be given time to assimilate the new information and integrate it thoroughly into their understanding of the world about them before any further complexity is introduced.

The sensory awareness curriculum area divides naturally into components which correspond to the senses of vision, hearing, touch, taste, and smell. (The kinaesthetic sense is included in the body image component of the movement curriculum.) In all the component areas the main aims will be:

to promote consistent response to change in the environment;

to encourage the ability to locate and direct attention towards the source of stimulation;

to promote selective attention to salient stimuli and thereby reduce distractibility;

to encourage the use of all the senses to the fullest extent available;

to encourage awareness of different properties and differentiation between modalities;

to increase acuity and the ability to discriminate within the same modality;

to promote integration of sensory information which will form the basis for understanding the surroundings.

THE VISUAL COMPONENT

This component is concerned with children's looking skills and the way vision is used to regulate their actions. It is important to increase the contrast between the visual properties of objects and materials and the surface or background against which they are presented. Activities may include the use of any of the following:

Objects, which are brightly coloured, reflective, or particularly favoured by individual children, to encourage visual attention and visually directed actions;

Moving objects, used on the table or floor, or at various levels and distances from the children, to encourage visual tracking and scanning, visually directed reach, and exploration, which can be activated by the adult or the children and can include mechanical toys, balls, rolling toys, bubbles, balloons, spinning toys, windmills, and many other visually attractive items that are readily available or easy to make;

Mirrors, which can be used to intensify the effect of objects, or to reflect the movements of the adult or the children;

Light, which can be used as a direct source of visual stimulation or to enhance the properties of other materials, for example: by using an area where the lighting level can be controlled, such as a dark corner or a cupboard; by enhancing the intensity of fluorescent colours by means of ultraviolet light which may attract the attention of children who do not otherwise react to visual stimuli; by using a table lamp to intensify the light level in a small working area, heighten the contrast between the materials being used and the background, and thus reduce the distraction of the surroundings; by illuminating transparencies made from coloured acetate sheets; or by providing high intensity visual information, through other light sources such as slide projectors, video screens, and torches, which can be used in various ways to encourage looking skills;

Free play materials, which can be used to focus children's attention and to encourage integration of vision with other senses, for example: by finger painting with fluorescent paints, which provides a highly visual activity with additional tactile sensations; or by pouring water, which combines visual, auditory, and tactile sensations;

Everyday objects and representations, such as miniatures or pictures, which provide opportunities for recognition and discrimination, form a part of daily activities such as having a drink, mealtimes, and washing, and can be used in early symbolic play.

THE AUDITORY COMPONENT

This component is concerned with hearing which is of immense importance to children. It provides them with information about the immediate surroundings, and extends the range of their awareness and understanding of the environment by giving them clues about events that occur beyond the limits of touch and vision. In addition, auditory awareness and selective attention to sound are essential pre-requisites for the development of receptive and expressive speech. Any deficit or distortion in these areas will have immense implications for children's intellectual and social development.

The difficulty of classroom testing for auditory impairment lies partly in the nature of children's responses and partly in the nature of the environment. Few schools have truly distraction-free areas, so that testing for response to sound usually takes place against a background of miscellaneous noises, some of which will be meaningful and within children's range of perception, and some of which will be meaningless or inaudible to them. Lack of any detectable response to specific sounds does not necessarily indicate inability to hear, since children may block out sounds if they are of no interest to them or if they are unintelligible or overwhelming in some respect. It is vitally important to establish the threshold at which individual children respond consistently to sound so that in the course of teaching the choice of sounds, whether speech or otherwise, can be based upon the pitch, intensity, and type that are audible to them and are most likely to attract and maintain their attention.

It is possible that there will be a very limited range of sounds to which children attach any meaning and to which they respond appropriately; but by increasing their awareness and responses to sound they may be encouraged to use hearing to greater effect in understanding their environment.

Virtually all activities incorporate auditory elements but there are some which emphasise auditory skills:

Structured sessions to promote listening skills, which are concerned with developing awareness and responses to sound through a selection of sound makers to elicit:

> *basic responses,* such as startle, eye-blink, or change of behaviour, on presentation of sounds of all kinds — including speech and other familiar sounds as well as a range of sound-makers of varying pitch and intensity — in different positions and distances, within and outside children's field of vision;

> *interest* in sound and *integration* of vision and touch with hearing in searching for and locating the source of sounds which have previously elicited a basic response;

> *exploration* of sound by using a range of actions to repeat or make new sounds either using the children themselves as a sound source, as in clapping, stamping, or babbling, or by using sound making objects:

> *discrimination* between different sounds, by matching identical sound makers.

All these activities provide opportunities for integrating sound with other senses, for example, by using visual and tactile cues to promote attention to and understanding of sounds and to encourage children to look, grasp, and use objects as well as listening to the sounds they make;

Environmental sounds are always present, and those which are significant to children can be enhanced and made more consistent, so facilitating recognition, discrimination, and the use of sound as a source of information about the surroundings; children's attention and understanding being guided by verbal comment or labelling by the adult, or by the use of touch cues, visual cues, or particular movements related to the sound, thereby helping children to associate sounds with objects, events, or pictures from which they originate, or to which they refer;

Music, a sound source which seems to have a fundamental appeal to almost everyone, can be used in many ways to encourage listening skills and to elicit responses, even when used by non-musical adults, in sessions such as music and movement, where the music imposes rhythm and continuity which is reflected in children's movements whether these are active or passive; or in activities where specific musical sequences are used to initiate and direct actions; or in action songs and musical games which provide a structure for simple actions, such as clapping, or for guiding children through various action sequences.

THE TACTILE COMPONENT

This component offers a very important means of gaining information for young children, and it remains particularly important for children with visual impairments and developmental delay. McInnes and Treffrey (1982) point out that "tactile" refers to sensory input which originates from any external area of the body and is not confined to the use of hands and fingers in gaining information from the surroundings. Even if children cannot use touch systematically themselves, they are constantly involved in tactile experiences: through the clothing they wear, the surfaces that support them, the objects which are in contact with any body part, and through direct physical contact with other people, especially carers.

If children are to gain the maximum amount of information possible from the sense of touch they must be able to tolerate a wide variety of tactile experiences on different parts of the body, and to locate the area of the body from which the sensations come, as well as to discriminate between different tactile stimuli.

Tactile sensations can be differentiated by general properties, such as duration, intensity, and location, and also by characteristics which are specific to the source of the stimulation. It is important to bear all these aspects in mind when planning activities which are likely to include:

Passive experience of tactile stimuli on different parts of the body, which are provided by the adult in a variety of ways, such as:

>   *direct contact* by touching, stroking, or massaging the hands and feet, limbs and body;

>   *applying various substances*, such as talcum powder, oils, soap, or sticky, wet, slimy, or gritty substances;

>   *different textures*, for example, fabrics such as velvet, netting, or hessian, or objects which are highly tactile, such as feely bags, pan scrubbers, loofahs, or brushes;

>   *vibration*, including vibrators or vibrating platforms used at variable speeds, and musical instruments, such as drums or cymbals;

Contrasting materials to emphasise and encourage discrimination of various properties:

>   *wet/dry* — sand, water, cloths, sponges;

>   *hot/cold* — various different drinks, hot water bottles, ice packs, warm or cold water;

>   *soft/hard* — various surfaces or objects, floor, carpet, bean-bag;

>   *heavy/light* — feely bags, bottles of water, bricks, balls;

Active exploration of objects and materials which vary in texture, temperature, weight, shape, movement, or solidity, and encourage actions such as grasping, stroking, fingering, or squeezing to identify the different properties, including:

>   *free play materials*, like water, sand, paper, clay, and dough, which offer very specific tactile experiences because of their texture, malleability, and impermanent forms;

>   *natural materials*, such as fir cones, leaves, twigs, grass,

conkers, and stones — although safety considerations are most important when using these materials;

solid objects, such as bricks, balls, and toys, which provide an infinite variety of permanent shapes combined with other properties;

fabrics and paper, including feely bags and every-day items which may be permanent or changeable in form.

Systematic use of touch cues, which give children information about their surroundings, and particularly about forthcoming events, through simple "vocabulary" — based upon the signing system used in the school — in which a touch cue to a particular part of the body has a specific meaning; for example, raising both hands when children are sitting may indicate that they should stand up; touching children on the shoulder (if *Makaton* (Walker, 1978) is generally used) may indicate that they are going to be taken to the toilet; touching the mouth may show that they are going to be offered food or drink; a specific touch may be used for "finished" or "all gone", and others may be used systematically in social interaction, such as when greeting or leaving.

THE TASTE AND SMELL COMPONENT

This component covers two sensory areas because they are closely linked. They produce less information about the environment than the other senses, but they can still be very important, particularly for children who have significant losses in other sensory areas. Children can use the sense of smell to identify places, such as the swimming pool, art room, home activities room, or riding stables; or to differentiate between well-known people.

In many schools meals are not cooked on the premises, and the aroma of cooking does not precede the mealtime. The food is sometimes served in such a way that children cannot distinguish individual flavours or textures. As a result they may refuse foods which are unfamiliar or which have a distinctive flavour, or they may become totally undiscriminating in food or drink. If a preference for certain foods or flavours can be established, these can be used in planning children's self-help programmes in eating and drinking. It is very useful to find out whether children prefer savoury or sweet foods as this can make a considerable difference when planning a feeding programme, and when teaching children to make considered choices, particularly at mealtimes.

The activities used to develop the senses of taste and smell might include:

Taste/smell sessions in the classroom, in which a variety of smells (such as coffee, curry, herbs, or scent) and a range of foods and drinks (which vary in flavour, texture, or temperature) are offered, with tiny amounts of food, like *Marmite*, peanut butter, or jam, being given on a spoon or spread onto cubes of toast or biscuits; and a variety of hot and cold drinks being offered, such as *Bovril*, fruit juices, coffee, and flavoured milk, to establish which they most enjoy; the children not being given too much strongly flavoured food or drink and being allowed enough time to empty the mouth before being offered a new flavour, so that the object of the exercise is not defeated by the flavours becoming mixed.

Mealtimes and drink times, which can be used to increase children's discrimination and enjoyment of foods, can also be used to allow them to smell the food before it is put into their mouths so that they gain some idea of what they are being offered and have some basis for deciding whether to accept or refuse it; this skill sometimes developing sufficiently for children to be able to indicate in advance whether they want a particular food or drink.

However extensive their impairments it is vital that children with profound handicaps should be helped to improve their sensory perception and maximise the use of any residual abilities. The activities used in the sensory awareness curriculum should be planned to provide a reactive environment with activities which can be predicted by the children, thereby encouraging the use of purposeful and goal directed behaviours which will enable them to influence and control their environment to the greatest possible extent.

Perceptual motor

In this curriculum model the perceptual motor area is treated as a core area because it emphasises the integration of the various senses and combines them with movement to produce complex action patterns. All forms of movement involve some sensory elements. The more precise, fine motor skills in particular require a considerable amount of sensory information to elicit, carry out, and monitor the purposeful actions with which children explore, manipulate, and control their environment.

The nature of movement is determined by the characteristics of external objects and events. An increasing degree of control is required to differentiate and refine the early global movement patterns and build up a repertoire of actions that are appropriate for specific situations and materials. Initially all the senses are important in eliciting action, but it is likely that vision, hearing, and proprioception will gradually predominate. If there is no visual impairment, visuo-motor activities will ultimately assume the greatest importance in guiding children's actions.

Much research has been carried out into the integration of vision with early manipulative behaviours (Bruner, 1974; Bower, 1977; Cratty, 1979). Early visual distractibility of infants is replaced by the ability to attend to visual stimuli, especially those with certain properties: movement; features resembling the human face; and patterns with good figure/ground differentiation. Tracking of moving objects and the ability to attend alternately to two different objects is necessary before visually directed reaching can develop. This opens up opportunities for children to investigate and manipulate objects in their immediate surroundings.

The development of accurate reach and grasp is well-documented, and occurs in a sequence of well-defined stages. The earliest reaching behaviour is triggered by a visual stimulus and is an undifferentiated swiping at the object, preceded by mouthing motions. Research has shown that there is expectation of contact with the object and, if this is not forthcoming, subsequent signs of distress. If the reach is successful and the object secured it is frequently brought to the mouth for oral exploration. An auditory stimulus can also trigger the reach and grasp action pattern, but Bower (1977) points out that sound contains far less information to help the child locate the object successfully and so the response does not persist, even in non-sighted children. Environmental sounds, however, do continue to be used to interpret events in the surroundings.

This all-in-one action pattern is followed by a stage in which the component elements are separated and children's actions are guided by looking alternately at the object and their own hand. Visual inspection of their own hands is an important prior phase, and Bower (1977) suggests that if children do not become familiar with the sight of them they will distract their attention from other objects and delay hand-eye coordination. The action of grasping is controlled by contact with the object, and the chances of successfully securing an object at this stage are much greater than previously. Further refinements occur, with adaptation of the grasp to match the properties of the object, which is then brought to the midline for exploration and manipulation.

The efficiency of manual exploration of objects depends upon the type of grasp and degree of control of the finger movements used. The palmar grasp allows turning and passing from hand to hand, thus facilitating visual inspection from all sides; but the use of the finger tips and finger-thumb opposition is necessary for more precise manipulation. The properties perceived by means of tactual inspection include rigidity, unity, stability, weight, texture, shape, and thickness. Children gradually become more able to adapt the strength of grip according to the size and weight of the object: initially they accommodate to weight after grasping the object, but later they adjust their grip in anticipation of the weight of familiar objects.

The next stage is when children begin to use an increasing number of action routines in examining and exploiting the properties of objects. These actions have been identified by Uzgiris (1967). They include shaking, banging, pulling and pushing, tearing, squeezing and crumpling, rubbing and stroking, and dropping and throwing objects. Bruner (1974) stresses the importance of mastery play which he describes as playful means-ends matching. This may involve a new object being fitted into as many routines as children have available, or a new act addressed to as many different objects as are available. Children who have motor impairments, or who have a severe loss of vision or hearing, will find participation in these activities extremely difficult or even impossible. Integration of sensory information and movement will have to be encouraged by means of aids and equipment which will exploit their residual abilities to the fullest extent possible, or by passive movement and careful management of the learning situation. Also, many children with profound handicaps, who could reach out and secure an object, lack the motivation to do so or, having acquired a very restricted number of movement routines which they use in interacting with their surroundings, have great difficulty in progressing to the next stage.

In this stage the properties of objects are exploited and the objects are used appropriately and purposefully, the children's actions being directed towards a definite goal. Once attained, the ability to use objects in meaningful relationships and to sequence actions to achieve a result allows children to occupy themselves productively without the constant intervention of an adult.

The combination of perception with movement encourages integration of information and the formation of concepts such as shape, size, weight, texture, and spatial and temporal relationships. This provides the basis for children to interpret events and situations and relate to them appropriately, and thus lays the foundation for the development of cognitive abilities.

The overall aims of the perceptual motor curriculum are:

to increase fine motor control and integration of sensory information and action patterns;

to encourage the acquisition of a repertoire of differentiated routines, for exploration and manipulation of the surroundings;

to promote the ability to organise and carry out a sequence of actions directed towards a goal.

More specific aims relate to the various component areas of fine motor control and occupation skills.

THE FINE MOTOR COMPONENT

This component is concerned with visual control in conjunction with hand and arm movements. Aims will be:

to establish head control in various orientations;

to establish occular control and the ability to attend visually to objects within the visual field;

to increase control of hand and arm movements and encourage development of manual dexterity;

to promote eye-hand coordination.

Some of the activities which can be used to contribute towards the achievement of these aims are:

Physiotherapy exercises and positioning, which assist head control and postural stability, and enable children to maintain a head position which allows visual attention;

Looking skills, in which brightly coloured objects, such as balls, mechanical toys, reflective surfaces, lights, and any other stimuli which are attractive to individual children, are used to encourage:

> *fixation* on a stationary object at all levels and distances within the visual field;

> *alternation of gaze* between two objects, or hand and object;

> *tracking* of slowly moving objects in all orientations — up and down, side to side, in a circle, diagonally;

> *convergence and divergence* on an object as it is moved slowly nearer and further away;

> *visual inspection* of own hands and objects in midline;

> *visual scanning* of surfaces and arrays of objects;

Mirror work, when a large mirror is used to enhance children's awareness of their own movements through the moving reflections; or a mirror at various angles is used to increase the visual effect produced by moving objects, such as a ball rolling across a mirror, or the reflection of a mobile or a mechanical toy;

Exploratory activities, in which similar materials are used to encourage active exploration, using one hand only or both hands carrying out the same or a complementary action, through:

> *voluntary grasp and release* of objects, using mature grip appropriate to the materials or task;

> *visually or auditorily guided reaching* to secure stationary and moving objects at various levels and distances;

> *manual exploration* of objects by passing from hand to hand, turning and rotating, fingering and poking, and carrying out a variety of actions on each object.

THE OCCUPATION SKILLS COMPONENT

This component is concerned with enabling children to acquire a repertoire of actions through which they can influence their environment and experience. It also seeks to help them integrate sensory information and simple actions into more complex sequences which will enable them to participate in other areas of the curriculum. The main aims, therefore, are:

to encourage the acquisition of a wide range of actions;

to promote integration of sensory information and actions;

to encourage awareness of the different properties of various stimuli and to form basic concepts;

to encourage the use of actions which are appropriate to the materials or task in hand;

to promote organised sequences of action directed towards a goal;

to maintain an activity to completion of task or attainment of goal.

Many activities can be used to work towards these aims. These include:

Exploratory activities, in which materials and objects with different attributes, such as sound toys, feely bags, mirrors, brightly coloured objects, and activity centres, are used to encourage children to use a number of different actions to achieve a variety of results;

Placing activities, in which objects are related in a variety of ways, such as putting them in and taking them out of containers, piling or stacking them, nesting, posting, threading, or fitting them together in various ways (as with *Stickle Bricks,* or *Lego*), or pattern making with pegboards, mosaics, and inset boards; these skills being essential prerequisites for matching and sorting activities, and the symbolic use of objects;

Imitation of actions carried out by adults or other children, either using objects or gesture, through structured sessions, activity songs, or drama games;

Creative activities, such as when using:

free play materials, the properties of the different materials encouraging different actions and various tools or equipment;

music, the instruments involving a wide range of actions, such as banging, shaking, pressing, stroking, and beating (employing various kinds of beaters for drums, chime bars, wood blocks) which produce different results, the rhythm of the music promoting sequencing and rhythm in the actions of the children;

art and craft, when mark makers such as felt pens, crayons and paint can offer a high-contrast visual medium to encourage purposeful actions and appropriate use of equipment; when clay and dough can encourage manipulative skills and use of tools; and collage can encourage various actions such as tearing, cutting, sticking, and the appropriate use of tools and materials;

drama, during which visual and auditory cues can signal multisensory experiences and sequences of action which children can anticipate and join in.

Cognitive

This curriculum area is concerned with the acquisition of basic skills which include the learning strategies and adaptive behaviours that allow effective interaction with the surroundings, and the broader understanding of physical and social contexts which will enable children to behave in a way which is appropriate and effective in a range of situations. This area is vitally important because of the difficulty the children have in making sense of their surroundings and the consequent limitation of incidental or spontaneous learning. Bailey (1983) comments that:

"it has been requisite to teach the children 'how to learn' and a marked proportion of individual needs have appeared in this area. If the children are to make any sense of their environment they must also attain an understanding of concepts relating to their environment".

It is convenient in this model to consider three component areas of the cognitive curriculum: basic skills, concept formation, and situational understanding. All three are essential if children are to attain any degree of autonomy. The main aims of this curriculum area are:

to establish attention control and the ability to concentrate on a task or activity;

to promote the acquisition of mental processes and strategies necessary for learning;

to encourage the acquisition of a repertoire of actions which will allow exploration, manipulation, and purposeful use of objects;

to facilitate the formation of basic concepts;

to promote symbolic development;

to promote understanding of the objects, events, and situations which children experience.

BASIC SKILLS

This component seeks to promote the mental processes and behaviour patterns which are prerequisites for learning in all areas of the curriculum, and which are usually acquired through play in early childhood.

It is common for children with profound handicaps to be highly distractible. Attention control is, therefore, likely to be a priority in the individual programmes of many children in the special class. Bower (1977) suggests that attention control is a combination of attentional capacity, which increases during the course of growth and development, and the amount of attention required by an object, which decreases with familiarity resulting from exposure to objects and events in the world.

Cooper, Moodley, and Reynell (1978) describe five stages in the development of attention control. It is most likely that the first three stages will be most relevant for children in the special class. In the first stage of extreme distractibility, children's attention is held momentarily by the dominant stimulus in the classroom; in the second stage, children can attend selectively to tasks of their own choice; and in the third stage they can transfer attention from one focus to another with the guidance of another person. Clearly, attention skills are involved in every activity undertaken, whether carried out alone or with an adult or peers, and it is important that children's attentional ability is considered in every situation from a structured teaching session to a period of free self-occupation. The intensity of the physical characteristics of the objects used with the children and the children's familiarity with them, as well as the teaching environment in general, will affect the degree of attention to the task which children will be able to sustain.

Many children with profound handicaps have a very restricted repertoire of actions which they use in their interaction with their surroundings. Often they do not develop the range of actions of which they are physically capable. It is common for them to use only two or three actions, such as mouthing, banging, or throwing, quite indiscriminately, with any object regardless of its properties. Although this is a normal stage of investigative behaviour it limits the amount of learning possible. It is therefore important that the children's repertoire of actions should be increased and used systematically to explore the surroundings, and that children should learn to differentiate between actions and use objects purposefully and appropriately.

As children's attention skills and repertoire of actions increase, they will develop more complex strategies in their interactions with the immediate surroundings. Search strategies, exploratory play, and imitation of others will all be used to discover and control their environment. If the environment is to have any meaning for children, they must be able to interpret the information it contains. Mental processes such as discrimination, memory, association, and categorisation, which enable children to select and organise such information, to generalise, and to predict outcomes, are all necessary.

CONCEPT FORMATION

This component is concerned with the acquisition of the basic concepts that are vital if children are to be able to construct a representation of the world upon which understanding and control of the environment is based.

The concept of object permanence is fundamental if the children are to have any appreciation of the environment which exists beyond the limits of their senses and range of movements. Where there are physical or sensory deficits this concept is even more important as it must be used to compensate for the restrictions imposed by the disabilities. The stages of development of the object concept identified by Piaget are well known and there are many sources which interpret his work (Ginsberg and Opper, 1979) as well as his own writings (Piaget, 1953; 1954). Later research has suggested alternative interpretations of the development of object permanence (Oates, 1979; Bower, 1977) but the importance of "the concept of objects as permanent entities with enduring and predictable characteristics (in providing) a corner stone for referential language, for social attachment, and for conceptual growth" is not disputed (Nelson, 1974).

Cause and effect relationships and differentiation of means from ends are also essential if children are to have any control over their surroundings and experiences. They must be able to act consistently in relation to people, objects, and situations. They must be able to use objects purposefully to attain a goal. Initially, they must associate actions — their own or other people's — with the consequences. As control of their own movements improves, unintentional or involuntary movements which are random or reflex will be superceded by intentional movements. This will allow children to repeat actions which have had a pleasurable result, or to imitate the actions of someone else; thus laying the foundation for the concept of causality. Ultimately, children's actions will become purposeful and directed towards a predetermined goal.

Bruner (1974) suggests that skilled actions include: intention, that "precedes, directs and provides a criterion for terminating an act"; structure and sequencing of the elements of the complete pattern of action; and feedback, which includes not only the observable result but also children's prediction as to what the result of their actions should be. As children's representation of the world becomes more complex, so the separation of means from ends can be extended and the purposeful and appropriate use of objects incorporated into the patterns of action.

Spatial and temporal relationships of people and objects within the environment are closely linked with the concepts of object permanence and causality. Knowledge of these will be acquired through interaction with the surroundings.

General concepts, such as shape, size, colour, texture, and function, which are based on the physical properties of objects, will enable children to identify items which are familiar to them. As they come into contact with similar items and attributes they will begin to generalise the concepts they have gained and to categorise and organise their surroundings and experiences into a coherent and predictable model of the world.

Symbolic development is vital if children's understanding of reality is not to be restricted to the immediate concrete environment. "The use of mental representations permits the child to transcend the constraints of space and time" (Ginsberg and Opper, 1979). There are many stages in symbolic development. These are probably most easily traced through the development of play, as increasingly abstract symbols are incorporated into action sequences ranging from simple imitation of familiar routines to fantasy sequences which go beyond children's direct experience.

Firm concepts relating to everyday objects and activities are necessary before symbolic development can take place. Initially objects are identified by their function and the actions which are involved in their use. Piaget (1953; 1954) considers imitation to be an essential element in symbolic development which is later internalised to form mental representations. Pretend play will involve recreating familiar situations using everyday objects. Small sized or miniature objects, such as dolls, cars, and animals, will be incorporated into more complex sequences of domestic or world play. As imaginative play develops, different people will be represented in role play and a wide range of situations created. One object will be used to represent a different object, and will be used according to the demands of the activity. Complex constructions will be created to enhance the course of the action.

Symbolic development is also evident in the process of acquiring a system of communication. Identification of objects by use, and direct actions to indicate need or interest, are succeeded by sounds or gestures with more precise meanings. As children begin to recognise and identify pictures, sounds, or gestures as representing objects, these can be used to represent the objects in their absence, thereby laying the foundation for the ability to communicate, whether by means of speech or some alternative system.

Every experience children have contains cognitive elements; but it is important to provide them with activities which offer opportunities to acquire and exercise cognitive skills which are appropriate to their level of operating. Exposure to a rich and stimulating environment, which encourages the development of mental processes in children who are not handicapped may be counterproductive for those with profound handicaps. Rostron and Sewell (1984) point out that, paradoxically, for these children the environment may be limited by too great a degree of complexity which is likely to produce confusion or even distress and may cause them to react inappropriately or to withdraw from the situation. Much cognitive processing may have to be done through the careful choice of materials and presentation of tasks to enable the children to appreciate the essential attributes of familiar objects and familiar contexts. This will enable them to use and extend their processing skills, to make associations and generalisations, and to form concepts relating to their surroundings. However, they must also have the opportunity to interact with the environment and to investigate the properties of both familiar and novel materials freely. It is unlikely that many children with profound handicaps will reach a high level of symbolic development, but it is still important to provide opportunities which encourage imitation and imaginative play, particularly if a formal system of communication is being taught.

Many of the activities used to promote acquisition of basic skills and early concepts will be those used in other areas of the curriculum, such as:

Looking and listening skills, to enhance visual and auditory attention and discrimination;

Tactile exploration, to encourage attention and discrimination through touch and manual investigation of objects;

Developmental movement, to help encourage attention to another person and then gradually to extend the sphere of attention to include the surroundings and more vigorous or exciting movements;

Exploratory activities, such as described in the perceptual motor area of the curriculum, to extend the range of actions used and to develop the concepts of object permanence, cause and effect, and concepts relating to the properties of the objects and materials provided, it being particularly important that children should be able to explore free play materials like wet and dry sand, water, and clay or dough, as well as solid objects, since free play materials differ significantly from most other materials in that they can change their form and have properties such as liquidity or malleability which other objects do not have and, because they are non-prescriptive in the ways they can be used, allow children to investigate and use them in endless ways;

Turntaking games, such as give and take, and activities such as hiding and finding objects, to establish joint attention on the object being used, and help children alternate attention between the adult and object.

Imitation sessions, to promote development at many different levels; for example, by simple modelling of actions on objects, such as pushing a car or dropping a ball, to increase the range of actions which children will use and so extend their exploratory skills; by more complex actions which relate two objects together, such as banging a drum with a stick, giving a biscuit to a doll, or relating a familiar object to oneself (like pretending to use a hairbrush), to encourage the use of simple symbolic behaviour; and by using gestures or imitating sounds to lay the foundation for the use of a formal system of communication;

Placing, matching, and sorting activities, varying from simple transfer of objects from one place to another, such as bricks into a box, to discrimination between similar objects on the basis of one or more attributes; matching and sorting, by colour, shape, size, picture, or any combination of these, being incorporated into placing activities;

Microelectronics, involving the use of switches for control of toys and equipment of varying complexity, from simple battery operated toys, lights, or cassette players to more complex, purpose-built toys and computers, facilitating acquisition of a very wide range of skills ranging from visual and auditory attention to early concepts such as cause and effect, means-end relationships and, at later stages, more complex cognitive skills such as discrimination, choice making, and problem solving.

Drama games, used at many levels, to sustain and extend children's attention, develop imitation, and promote generalisation of the basic cognitive skills of recognition and association, anticipation, sequencing, differentiation of responses, and participation.

Higher level drama sequences, to encourage imagination through symbolism, special or fantastic situations outside children's everyday circumstances being set up to allow them to experience the build up of tension within a controlled and safe situation.

SITUATIONAL UNDERSTANDING

This component is concerned with children's ability to appreciate the significance of physical and social contexts and their awareness of the implications of these in relation to the social culture in which they live. It is an essential part of the curriculum if children are to be enabled to make decisions, use their skills and abilities in an appropriate and effective way, and exert some degree of control over their experiences.

At the simplest level children must have some expectation of what is likely to happen in certain places or when particular actions are carried out, and thus be able to understand and participate in everyday routines such as mealtimes, toileting, classroom activities, or going shopping. Special occasions, such as weddings, and events which recur, such as birthdays, sports days, and holidays, involve social customs which children can recognise. This will help them to participate in such activities as members of a group.

The activities in this component seek to compensate for the restricted experience and limitation of choice imposed on children with profound handicaps by their disabilities:

Broadening of experience, which helps children to construct a realistic idea of the society in which they live, it being necessary to emphasise to them the essential features by which they can recognise various situations and events; birthdays, for example, being distinguished by a cake, candles, balloons, and a "birthday" boy or girl; shopping by a basket, purse, and list;

Social and domestic routines, which can be replicated within the school, and which will be encountered by the children at home, such as washing up, preparing meals, making tea, writing and posting letters, and giving gifts, will help children to form concepts about these activities;

Understanding of the wider community, which can be aided through visits to public places, such as shops, cafés, parks and gardens, and by watching or using different forms of transport as well as by attending traditional seasonal events, such as bonfire night and religious festivals, will allow children to participate in activities within the community, thus increasing their understanding and helping them to see themselves as members of a wider society.

Communication

Communication is of prime importance in the curriculum. It is inherent in every activity undertaken with the children and the establishment of some form of interaction is an essential prerequisite for teaching. Communication is also vital for the personal development of the children as it enables them to express and to satisfy their physical needs, their need for social interaction, and their need for competence in understanding and organising their surroundings. These needs create the motivation for children to acquire and use an effective system of communication.

In a survey of 817 children in "special care" classes, Evans and Ware (1987) found that less than 20 per cent were reported to use any formal means of communication. Of the children who did, 16 per cent used speech and fewer than four per cent used an alternative system or combination of systems. Of the 20 per cent or so who had some means of communication, nearly half used fewer than 10 words or signs.

Since most children in special classes are non-verbal, and very few have more than a rudimentary means of communication, much work in the communication curriculum will be at the pre-verbal level. This is the stage in which the interactive patterns and underlying cognitive processes are established, in preparation for the use of more complex receptive and expressive systems involving the use of established conventions and orthodox symbols. Many of the children in special classes have sensory or motor impairments or such severe learning difficulties that they will not be able to use orthodox systems and any early interactive exchanges that are established may remain their only channel of communication.

The ability to communicate depends upon: establishing reciprocal interaction with others; gaining a concept of communication as a means of giving and receiving information; and employing a system that uses conventions and codes which will be understood by others. In addition, children must have the motivation, the intention, and the need to communicate if anything more than the most rudimentary expression of their feelings and requirements is to be achieved.

In order to be able to communicate effectively children must be able to produce consistent behaviour which can be accurately interpreted by others. They must also be able to attend to others and interpret their actions and speech. Establishing a means of communication will depend upon each child's individual repertoire of actions and stage of cognitive development, which will give an indication of their ability to understand and use a systematic code, whether this is speech or some alternative system.

The major elements involved in acquiring a system of communication include the interaction patterns and cognitive processes which will facilitate both receptive communication, that is an ability to understand others, and a systematic means of expressive communication, which will enable children to make their needs and wishes known to others. These four parallel strands can be regarded as the component areas of the communication curriculum and they are all closely linked. It follows that all four must be included when planning a communication programme for children who are operating at an early developmental level. It is sometimes assumed that once an alternative communication system is introduced children will have the means to communicate, without sufficient consideration being given to whether they have gained the underlying social and cognitive skills to enable them to do so.

The main aims of the communication curriculum will therefore reflect all these areas and will be:

to encourage responsiveness to the presence of others and establish reciprocal interaction patterns;

to promote consistent behaviours in relation to people and objects;

to establish understanding and systematic use of communicative behaviours;

to build a repertoire of signals related to needs, preferences, interests, ideas, and feelings;

to establish a means of communication which will enable children to exchange information with others and exert some degree of control over their surroundings and experiences.

INTERACTION PATTERNS

This component seeks to establish the intention to communicate, and the capacity for reciprocal interaction through movements or vocalisations which follow rules or conventions which allow sustained communication to be maintained, either with individuals or within a group.

Initially children must learn that "coincidental" behaviours in reaction to internal or external changes will result in a consistent response from others; then, that this result can be achieved intentionally, by producing the behaviours which elicit the desired response; and finally, that these behaviours can be used systematically, according to rules or conventions which are understood by both partners in the exchange.

Synchronisation of the behaviour of both partners is necessary before effective interaction can take place. The process is initiated in situations of direct contact in which an adult is "tuned in" to a child and the actions of both are synchronised in a joint activity focused on the child's responses. At this stage children regulate the interaction unintentionally as the adult imputes meaning to their behaviours, such as bodily movements or vocalisations which are reactions to the immediate situation, and responds appropriately. By repeating certain behaviours children gain expected responses and, once they have learned this, they can deliberately influence the course of their interactions.

Reciprocal interaction is encouraged by adults allowing time for children to respond, and prompting or "filling in" if no response is forthcoming. During turntaking interaction, whether through actions as in physical games, objects as in give and take or hiding games, or vocalisations in conversations, adults will be using non-verbal behaviours, such as eye-contact, direction of gaze, and body movements, to maintain the interaction sequences and sustain the children's attention. Children will respond and incorporate these behaviours into their own repertoire so that ultimately they can initiate, maintain, and terminate interactions on an equal basis.

Interaction patterns can be established through various channels which depend upon the children's level of cognitive development and degree of attention control:

Direct interaction, which is the most immediate way of communicating, demands the simplest form of attention control — attention to one other person without any intervening object or event;

Interaction through objects, which becomes possible as children's attention and sphere of interest widens, can be encouraged by following the children's gaze and elaborating upon the object that is attracting attention, thus establishing joint attention upon an object and the possibility of creating mutual understanding;

Interaction through symbols, which only becomes possible when children can associate representations with objects or concepts to which they refer, enables the understanding and systematic use of symbolic representations, integrated into interaction patterns regulated by commonly recognised rules or conventions, and makes possible an infinitely complex and flexible system of communication.

COGNITIVE PROCESSES

This component is fundamental to the other three components of the communication curriculum. It includes:

Attention control, which is vital for developing the sychronised interaction patterns already described and for establishing joint attention on objects or events in the surroundings which are the focus of communicative exchanges;

Concept formation, which is essential for establishing: mutual understanding of objects and events in the environment, upon which the exchange of information is based; cause-effect relationships so that children can begin to relate their own actions and those of other people to the consequences of those actions; and differentiation of means from ends, so that communicative behaviours can be used purposefully to achieve a predetermined result through an effective system of communication;

Symbolic development, which is necessary for understanding and using all but the most basic forms of communication, involving the ability to associate words, signs, or symbols with the objects or concepts which they represent.

These cognitive processes have already been discussed in the cognitive skills area of the curriculum (pp 131-138).

RECEPTIVE COMMUNICATION

This component is concerned with enabling children to perceive and interpret the actions and behaviour of others, and to build a receptive vocabulary of signals which they can recognise and understand.

Cues of various kinds are available which can enable children to interpret other people's attempts to communicate. During the stage when interaction patterns are being established, daily routines and activities will be accompanied by comments and other communicative behaviours on the part of the adult. Essential meanings will be emphasised by the use of exaggerated facial movements and repetition of key words that are significant to the children and the activity. When the stage of interacting through objects is reached, routines and conventions involving familiar items will help to establish knowledge of their functions and, at the same time, association of the objects with the actions involved in their use. Mutual understanding of the significance of certain people, objects, and events, and their association with specific actions, signs, two dimensional symbols, and speech, will allow them ultimately to be referred to, whether physically present or absent, by the symbols which represent them.

The context in which communication takes place can also give children cues for interpreting what is being communicated. Some children become so expert at interpreting contextual situations that their ability to do so conceals an underlying lack of understanding of the communication system that is being used.

There are several channels through which children can receive information from others. Ability to perceive and understand conventional forms of communication depends upon the distance senses of hearing and vision; but for children with significant impairment of either or both of these senses, as well as in the earliest stages of establishing meaning through actions, other channels have to be used, and the senses of touch and proprioception assume great importance. The main channels of communication will be:

Physical cues, which are the simplest means of communication, involving the use of touch and passive movements of different parts of the body as cues to convey meaning — such as personal signs used to identify children or adults, informal signs which prepare children for some forthcoming change in their situation, or conventional signs or gestures adapted from a communication system such as *Makaton* (Walker, 1978; 1981) — all of which can be used to give children specific information and directions, or to provide additional cues when other systems are being used; this form of communication being fairly restricted in the range of meanings which it can convey, and dependent upon the extent of the children's acquisition of a realistic body image and their ability to differentiate between the cues given;

Vision, which is essential if children are to pick up and interpret the non-verbal cues which accompany speech, the gestures and signs used in orthodox signing systems such as *British Sign Language*, *Makaton*, or *Paget Gorman* (Kiernan, Reid and Jones, 1982) and the meaning of two dimensional systems which use pictures or symbols, such as *Rebus*, *Blissymbolics*, *Makaton symbols* (Peter and Barnes, 1982) and *Sig symbols* (Jones and Cregan, 1986);

visual attention, discrimination, and memory all being vital if any of these systems are to be the predominant means of communication:

Hearing, which is most important if speech is to be the predominant means of communication, requiring selective attention, memory skills, and discrimination of a wide range of speech sounds as vital elements needed for interpretation of words and the accompanying features of pitch, intonation, and rhythm.

It is very difficult to assess accurately the sensory impairments of children with profound handicaps. In view of this, and because of the relatively high incidence of such impairment in this group, the system of "total communication" — the combined use of objects, signing, pictures, and speech — is often advocated (Jago, Jago, and Hart, 1984). This affords children every possible cue that may help them attribute meaning and understanding to the words and actions of others.

EXPRESSIVE COMMUNICATION

This component seeks to encourage consistent behaviours on the part of the children in relation to people, objects, and events. These behaviours are ultimately differentiated and elaborated into a repertoire of appropriate signals which children can use to express their needs, preferences, interests, ideas, and feelings as the basis for a conventional system of communication which can be understood by others.

The intended purpose will determine the content of each communicative exchange. Motivation will be derived from children's needs: for survival, which is met through satisfaction of their physical needs; for social interaction and emotional security; and for understanding of and a degree of control over their experiences. It is important that adults who are sensitive to children's needs should not pre-empt their expression of them by anticipating and providing for all their wants. This removes the motivation for children to acquire and use communicative skills, and inadvertently prevents them from satisfying their need to develop competence and control.

There are several analyses of the functions of communication (Halliday, 1973; Kiernan and Reid, 1986) which have many common elements. The functions listed below seem to be the ones most appropriate to the communication needs of children with profound handicaps which should be incorporated into the curriculum:

Satisfaction of needs, which relates to children's physical survival and quality of life, requires children to have a means of indicating their physical state, such as pain, hunger, thirst, fatigue, cold, discomfort, or distress, as well as an ability to understand and respond to enquiries about their needs from other people;

Control of the environment, which is particularly important for children whose physical or intellectual limitations prevent them from organising and changing their surroundings or influencing their experiences directly, adults being used as agents to make things happen or to give them assistance when necessary, requires children to develop a means of attracting attention and requesting action as well as the ability to protest about, or refuse to participate in, unwanted situations;

Regulating interpersonal interaction, which is similar in some ways to the controlling function, but which is directly interpersonal, requiring children to develop behaviours which will allow them to initiate, maintain, or terminate interaction sequences at will and to be able to interpret and respond appropriately to similar behaviours when shown by other people;

Personal expression, which is concerned with children's interests in and understanding of their surroundings, and requires children to be able to express feelings of pleasure or displeasure in objects or events, make comments on the surroundings, or on present, past, or future events, and generally to express personal interests, preferences, ideas, or feelings, being able to label people, objects, and events which are particularly significant to them, and to express personal views about them;

Understanding and representing reality, which seeks to develop and extend children's competence in various situations, children needing to acquire information beyond that available from their immediate environment by asking questions, and giving and receiving information, this requiring them to be able to form concepts and establish shared meanings with other people.

The systems children use to communicate will not necessarily be the same as those used by others to communicate with them. The choice of system will depend upon their abilities and whether they have any communicative behaviours on which an orthodox communication system can be built.

Consistent and systematic behaviours develop gradually. In the earliest stages, when children learn to use actions purposefully to gain certain responses they use generalised behaviours, such as reaching, pointing, or looking, to indicate desire for an object or to direct the other person's attention to it. They develop from this stage to one where they can differentiate, and employ a range of actions with specific meanings related to their experiences and requirements. As they begin to recognise visual and auditory representations of objects and events, in the form of gestures, pictures, sounds, and words, these more precise modes of communication may supplement or replace the earlier behaviours used in interactive exchanges, enabling an orthodox system of communication to be established. Speech will always be the preferred system of communication, but for children who are profoundly handicapped it is likely that it will have to be supplemented with or replaced by the use of signs or symbols, depending upon the individual abilities and range of actions available to them. A combined system, using all possible channels of communication, may be necessary to allow children the greatest range of expression.

Children's vocabulary will be determined by the function their communications are intended to fulfil, and the meanings they intend to convey. There are lists available of the most commonly used words (Locke, 1985; Gilham, 1979), some of which might form the basis for the general vocabulary used in the communication curriculum. However, part of every child's vocabulary will be highly individual, reflecting each one's personality and background, and including words and names of people and objects, which have particular significance for them as individuals. It is important to bear in mind children's chronological age, and to encourage use of words or meanings which are appropriate to their peer group as well as those which are personally important.

Many elements of the communication curriculum are common to both the receptive and expressive components, but the means of understanding and the means of expressing will not necessarily be the same. It is important to identify deficits in both areas of communication and then to decide which channel or system is most likely to be used successfully in each.

It is easy to assume that if children do not respond appropriately it is because they lack understanding; but it may be because they are unable to perceive the signals accurately owing to a sensory impairment; or because they cannot produce the expected responses consistently. Conversely, children who are socially responsive and who have the ability to pick up cues from other people, may give the impression of having a higher level of comprehension than is actually the case, and this can lead to unrealistic expectations of them.

All systems require some physical involvement, whether this is the precise control of mouth and speech organs necessary to produce intelligible speech, the fine control of arm and hand movements used in sign systems such as *Makaton, Paget Gorman* or *British Sign Language,* or the ability to indicate manually, by eye-pointing, or by some other means, when using a symbol system such as *Rebus, Blissymbolics,* or *Makaton symbols* (Peter and Barnes, 1982) and *Sigsymbols* (Jones and Cregan, 1986).

Many children with profound handicaps have severe physical impairments which make expressive communication extremely difficult for them to achieve. If their voluntary movements are severely restricted some kind of electronic aid may be used to help them to communicate. If so it is important that the means of expression be made as easy as possible. The children can then concentrate on the content and meaning of their communication rather than the operation of the equipment, and thus be more likely to communicate successfully.

Although the component areas of the communication curriculum have been discussed separately, in actual practice they are so closely linked that activities which involve communication inevitably incorporate elements of them all. Clearly, interaction at some level takes place throughout the day whenever children receive attention, whether individually or in a group, and a major part of the communication curriculum is therefore incorporated into the general activity of the special classroom. However, unless classroom activities are used consciously as opportunities for learning, and the aims for each individual child borne in mind, they will not be effective learning situations because of the difficulties that the children have in interpreting and organising their experiences. Language used by the adults must be simplified and structured, and the key words or meanings must be emphasised and repeated; particularly when the language is being used directly with the children to regulate or comment upon an activity. It is also important, however, for children to hear ordinary speech, with normally flowing rhythms, pitch, and intonation so that they can learn to interact in a conversational manner. The meaning of the words is incidental to the social interaction which is maintained by the language patterns.

Structured teaching of communication skills is essential in every child's programme. Individual or small group teaching is necessary for children to acquire the prerequisite skills and to build a functional vocabulary. When planning a communication programme it is important to bear in mind the normal course of development. This will assist selection of activities at an appropriate level, thus offering the children the greatest opportunity to acquire and practise communicative skills.

The early development of verbal communication is well documented (Cooper, Moodley, and Reynell, 1978; Jeffree and McConkey, 1976; Deich and Hodges, 1977) and there are many sources of suggestions for activities to use in promoting language development and the prerequisite skills (Kiernan, Jordan, and Saunders, 1978; Cunningham and Sloper, 1978; Simon, 1986). Commercially produced language programmes, such as *Living Language* (Locke, 1985), *Portage* (Bluma, Shearer, Frohman and Hilliard, 1976; White and East, 1984), and the *Derbyshire Language Scheme* (Masidlover and Knowles, 1977) are available, but few of these are appropriate at the very early stages of communication. As communication is essentially a dynamic and creative process it must be related to the context in which it takes place and it must be relevant to the children and their partner or partners in the communication process. Any language scheme should be used as a source of ideas from which individual programmes can be devised, rather than as a definitive programme.

General information on alternative systems is also available (Peter and Barnes, 1982; Jones and Cregan, 1986; Tebbs, 1978) and literature, teaching manuals, and materials for the different systems can be obtained from educational suppliers. Most schools for children with severe learning difficulties use the *Makaton* sign system (Walker 1978; 1981), but there is less concensus about the use of symbol systems. It is often felt that a communication system which complements the signing system used in school may be the most practical. If this is to be useful beyond the confines of school and in later life, however, consideration should be given as to which system is most likely to be understood at home, in the community, or in the centres which the children are likely to attend.

Many activities suggested for other areas of the curriculum offer opportunities for teaching early communication skills. The close physical interaction involved in movement activities encourages synchronisation of action and promotes reciprocal and supportive routines. *Sherborne movement* (Sherborne, 1979) is flexible enough to accommodate children's needs for direct interaction at appropriate levels. Music and movement and a variety of drama games also provide opportunities for children to coordinate actions with increasingly complex rhythms and tempo, and at the same time to progress from interaction with one partner to participation in group activities. All movement activities incorporate an element of body awareness. This is essential for children who must rely on physical cues or passive signing as their main channel for receptive communication. Many suggestions for activities are included in the section on the body image component of the movement curriculum (pp 115-117).

Activities for promoting looking and listening skills are included in the visual and auditory components of the sensory awareness curriculum (pp 119-122). Other activities, which involve visual or auditory discrimination (matching, sorting, and sequencing) are necessary to improve selective attention to the spoken word and discrimination of speech and environmental sounds, as well as for recognition, discrimination, and selection of signs or symbols if this kind of system is to be used.

The perceptual-motor area of the curriculum also suggests activities which promote looking and listening skills, and integration of these into exploratory activities which will enable children to form basic concepts about objects and materials. Interaction of children and adults through objects establishes joint attention and mutual understanding of objects which are significant to the children. This can be extended by the use of small apparatus such as bean bags, balls, and sticks in movement activities to encourage body awareness and fine motor skills at the same time.

Imitation games can be effective in establishing reciprocal interaction. In the early stages the adult imitates the children's behaviour, thus encouraging repetition of that behaviour and setting up turntaking sequences of action. Variations on the children's actions, and new actions, can gradually be introduced by the adult as the children's skill in imitation increases. Such imitation can become the precursor to learning a formal sign system. Imitation of actions modelled by the adult which involve the use of objects can help to extend the children's range of actions and help establish mutual understanding of the functions of the objects. Ultimately, imitation may be used spontaneously by children in problem solving and imaginative play sequences.

As previously mentioned, electronic aids may be necessary to enable some children to communicate. It is essential that the switches and equipment provided match their physical and cognitive abilities. Sophisticated computer systems which involve discrimination and choices are likely to be too complex for children with profound handicaps for whom a simpler system involving a board or screen on which a number of symbols are displayed is likely to be more suitable. Children select the required symbols by operating a switch. It will therefore first be necessary to teach them switch control, perhaps initially to activate a simple toy, and to introduce the communication system only when they have mastered this.

It can be seen that the communication curriculum is so closely linked with all the other curriculum areas that, apart from specific teaching of vocabulary, it is impossible to separate them. It is important, therefore, that all activities are presented in a way which enhances the opportunities for acquiring communicative skills whilst encouraging development in other areas.

Independence

A high degree of dependence on others for satisfaction of personal needs is probably the most universal and obvious characteristic of children with profound handicaps. This dependence and the concomitant management problems are both time and energy consuming. It is not surprising that independence skills is one of the most frequently mentioned areas of the curriculum (Ouvry, 1983; Evans and Ware, 1987).

It can be difficult to think in terms of independence for children with the most severe impairments, particularly those with physical disabilities which severely restrict their range of actions. Personal independence involves the physical ability to perform self-help skills and the ability to make decisions in order to exert some degree of control over the environment and experiences. In practice, the curriculum is often heavily biased towards the acquisition of self-help skills, particularly in toileting and eating and drinking because of the implications for management at home and at school. Nevertheless, it is important to make definite provision for development of decision making and environmental control and not to leave these to occur incidentally during the course of day-to-day classroom activities. Given the chance, children may be able to achieve a degree of success in one area while remaining almost totally dependent in others.

The main aims of the independence curriculum, therefore, will be to develop self-help and environmental control, and these will form the components of this part of the curriculum.

SELF HELP

This component is concerned with the acquisition of skills involved in eating and drinking, dressing and undressing, washing and grooming, and toileting. Bailey (1983) observes that many children "require to learn the basics of life in order to maintain life itself, and make it more comfortable and satisfying". Apart from maintaining life, achievement in any area of self-help will also maintain dignity and allow children to develop a positive self-concept and sense of worth.

Children's appearance is particularly important if they are to be readily accepted into wider social groups and to have the opportunity to become participating members of society. Problems of hygiene and cleanliness — often associated with excessive dribbling, incontinence, or behaviours such as finger sucking — are common among children with profound handicaps and can prevent them from being acceptable to others. This is detrimental to the development of self-esteem.

The self-help component must seek to achieve the maximum possible independence in personal care and development of a positive self-concept and sense of worth. Its aims will be for children to learn:

to tolerate, cooperate, and participate in activities of daily living as far as the limitations imposed by their disabilities permit;

to develop awareness of, and take responsibility for, their own personal needs;

to improve their personal appearance by reducing unacceptable habits or behaviour.

Eating and drinking

There are many sources of information about feeding (Warner, 1981; Anderson, 1983) and all paramedical disciplines can offer guidance on development of eating and drinking skills, advise on appropriate techniques, and assist in planning feeding programmes.

Eating problems may relate to: the mechanics of feeding, the sequence of actions involved, or lack of motivation. Persistence of early reflexes, such sucking, gagging, or biting, will prevent the development of mature eating patterns. Children may be unable to carry out the sequence of actions involved in picking up food (or spoon) and putting it in the mouth, they may be disinterested in food, or they may reject food as a matter of course.

Successful feeding programmes depend upon accurate assessment of the development stage the children have reached and of the nature of their particular problems followed by introduction of appropriate techniques to overcome their difficulties and encourage better eating patterns. Particular care must be given to positioning, both of children and adults, since this affects the efficiency and safety of the eating process. The right aids are also important. Apart from seating there are many kinds of specially adapted cups, plates, and cutlery available; these should be chosen to suit each child's needs.

Wherever possible, programmes for individual children should be carried out by the same person over a period of time. The adult will then know the correct seating arrangements, aids, and techniques to use with each child and will know when it is appropriate to encourage them to eat or drink more, when they are no longer hungry or thirsty, or whether they dislike certain types of food or drink.

Eating and drinking is a source of pleasure for most people. It should be so for children with profound handicaps, even if they are totally dependent on others to supply their needs and wants in this area. Apart from the mid-day meal, there are other activities within school which can contribute towards the development of eating and drinking skills:

Taste and smell sessions, particularly important for children who need their food finely chopped or mashed and who may have difficulty distinguishing individual smells and flavours of different foods, can make use of many foods and household substances which have a strong aroma, such as coffee, herbs and spices, fruit, perfume, talcum powder, or cleaning fluids, or the phials of common smells, such as lawn mowings, wood smoke, and others which are rather less palatable contained in a commercially available odour kit*; the tasting of a variety of foods and drinks allowing adults to form an idea of children's preferences for subsequent use at mealtimes to encourage good eating habits, and children to become accustomed to different textures and types of flavours such as sweet or savoury, bland or strong, different textures of foods also being introduced; it being very important to give very small amounts of strong flavoured foods and to allow enough time, or give a drink of water, between flavours;

Morning or afternoon drinks, which offer ideal opportunities for carrying out drinking programmes and should be seen as teaching periods rather than "care", can be used to improve mouth control and the ability to manage a cup, and can provide experience of a variety of drinks and so allow children to exercise choice; various accompanying snacks being offered for the same reason as well as to encourage finger feeding;

Home activities, which can be held regularly in the housecraft room, can offer the chance to taste and smell different ingredients separately and then eat or drink the results of simple cooking activities, such as toast with various spreads, instant desserts, scrambled eggs, and hot or cold drinks, the smell of the cooking process possibly encouraging reluctant eaters to taste the results;

Desensitisation or *stimulation of the muscles* of the tongue and mouth, carried out on the advice and under the guidance of a speech therapist or physiotherapist, can help children control the muscles involved in eating and drinking and may help improve personal appearance by reducing dribbling and achieving lip closure.

---

*This kit, called the *Avon Fragrance Demonstrator,* is available from *RNIB, 224 Great Portland Street, London W1N 6AA.*

Continence

Control of bowel and bladder functions are an extremely important aspect in development of personal dignity and acceptability of the children as members of a group. Incontinence inevitably curtails children's freedom to participate in all that the community has to offer. Its implications in terms of management, hygiene, time, and expense are such that toilet training must be a priority area for teaching.

Very few children with profound handicaps are likely to achieve complete independence in toileting, since they must first be aware of their needs, then be able to make appropriate decisions relating to these needs, and finally be able to carry out the necessary actions. Even if complete independence is not possible because of the limitations imposed by their disabilities some degree of independence may be achieved in one or more of these elements.

There are many stages in achieving independence in toileting and, correspondingly, many programmes for promoting independence. However, the main aims must be to help children:

to become accustomed to being in a clean and dry state;

to achieve a degree of control of bowel and bladder functions;

to take responsibility for their own toileting needs and to communicate or attend to these needs appropriately.

Before planning individual toilet routines for the children it is necessary to assess each one's current level of development, discover whether they have any regular patterns already established, and find out if they show any behaviours, such as fretting or fidgeting, to indicate the need for toileting. This will involve frequent and accurate checks over a period of time and the use of recording charts to show any regularity in timing or frequency upon which individual routines can be based.

If children are eventually to achieve any success it is vital that they are comfortable and relaxed on the toilet. Suitable seats which they are accustomed to and can associate positively with the toileting process are essential if they are ever to learn to use the toilet appropriately. All children, even those who appear to be unaware of their bowel or bladder functions, should be kept clean and dry as far as possible. This means checking and changing whenever necessary, both for reasons of hygiene and also to accustom them to the dry state so that they are more likely to develop an awareness of their own functions, even if at first this is after the event. Association between the toileting process and bowel and bladder function can thus be encouraged. Such an association may be established more quickly if children show by some specific behaviour, such as fidgeting, restlessness, or crying, that they are aware of their needs or functions, either before or after the event, if it results in them being changed or taken to the toilet. It may then be possible to convert these generalised behaviours into an orthodox signal, which can be verbal, a gesture, or a symbol, which they can use to communicate this awareness to another person.

Once children begin to achieve some control they will be able to begin to use the toilet appropriately when put on at suitable times. At this stage it is particularly important for each one's idiosyncratic pattern to be followed so that the demands made on them are not too great for the amount of control they have achieved, and success can be regularly reinforced.

When children have achieved a degree of reliability they should be encouraged to take responsibility for deciding when to go to the toilet, either by being asked whether they need to go and the adult abiding by the answer given or, if they are capable of attending to their own needs independently, by leaving them to make the decision when to go without prompting. Even when children are reliable in familiar settings, however, it may be necessary to intervene when in unfamiliar surroundings or before going somewhere where facilities may not be available.

It is important that the toileting routine carried out in class is not so rigid that children have no opportunity to exercise any control over their toileting needs. It is essential for the dignity of children who have achieved some degree of control that they should be given every opportunity and assistance to be continent. Systematic recording is essential in the early stages of toilet training to reveal patterns, to monitor changes, and to record successes in using the toilet and achieving continence (see Figures 12 and 13, p156). Long-term charts can be made up from weekly charts to show gradual changes over longer periods of time. These can be very useful when reviewing toileting programmes and planning classroom routines.

Dressing

This highly complex activity makes great demands upon physical

NAME: ....

Week beginning	Arrival	Mid-Morning	Before Lunch	After Lunch	Early Afternoon	Home
Mon.						
Tues.						
Wed.						
Thurs.						
Fri.						

This chart allows for toileting six times during the school day, but children should be taken to the toilet only at the times appropriate to their individual needs. A more detailed chart (see Figure 13) may be necessary initially to establish each child's individual pattern of needs.

FIGURE 12. Toileting chart

NAME: .... WEEK BEGINNING ....

Monday		Tuesday		Wednesday		Thursday		Friday	

Key: Dry - D Wet - W Soiled - X   Used: Bladder - √ Bowels - B

On this chart the time is recorded in the left hand box and the result in the right hand box under each day.

FIGURE 13. Chart to establish each child's individual pattern of toileting needs

control, agility, and strength. It also requires the perceptual and intellectual skills needed to recognise different garments and sequence the actions involved in successfully putting on or removing them. Many children with profound handicaps will find some, if not all, elements beyond their capability. Even so, they can be helped to accept and cooperate in the dressing process. A relaxed person, who does not resist the handling which is inevitable in being dressed and can tolerate various positions, will be much easier to dress than one who resists.

Happily, many children can participate actively in the process to some extent; for them the technique of backward chaining is particularly appropriate. Some children will only be able to hold out an arm or leg, or push into a sleeve or shoe when asked, but some will be able to pull off a sock which has been pushed down to the toe, pull off the last coat sleeve, or pull a jumper or shirt over their head. As well as assisting in dressing, the process will be increasing their awareness of the relationship of their limbs to their body and thus enhancing their body image.

The most obvious aspect of dressing is the physical act of putting clothes on or taking them off, but there are other aspects in which children may be able to achieve a degree of independence even if they are not able to participate actively in the dressing process itself. These include:

recognition of their own personal items of clothing, particularly those which are distinctive and used daily, such as coats, shoes, or gloves;

recognition of different types of garments and their association with different parts of the body;

recognition of other people's garments;

awareness of relative size of clothes in relation to themselves, adults, other children, or dolls;

recognition of clothes which are appropriate to special occasions or activities, such as parties, swimming, physical education sessions, or to various weather conditions — summer and winter, rain or sun.

Another aspect, which is very important for personal development, is the ability to express preference for types of clothing and colours. This can be used to encourage children to make considered choices and to promote their self-awareness and positive self-concepts.

There are many occasions in the school curriculum when dressing skills can be incorporated into other activities:

before or after movement sessions or swimming;

when putting on overalls for "messy" sessions;

when stripping off for water or sand play;

in dressing up sessions or doll play;

and as a regular part of the toileting programme since it is essential, if children are to achieve independence in this, that they can deal with their own clothing competently.

There are other activities which can be undertaken with the children which, while not directly involving dressing skills, can help to promote a realistic body image and the movements needed in dressing and undressing. Directed movement, and activities using hoops, quoits, or bands, can improve the physical skills needed by the children.

Washing and grooming

These activities make complex demands upon children. Few pupils with profound handicaps will become entirely competent in these areas. They are, however, extremely important both in terms of hygiene and because of the effect they have upon personal appearance, dignity, self-esteem, and acceptability to others. The curriculum should seek to encourage in children the maximum possible degree of independence in personal hygiene and an interest in presenting a well-groomed appearance.

There are some problems, dribbling and finger sucking being particularly common, which can prevent children from being readily accepted by others and which can restrict their opportunities to participate in social situations. Behaviours of this kind are notoriously difficult to control. Effort should be made to reduce them by helping children distinguish between being wet or dry. This can be done by encouraging them to close the mouth and swallow, or wipe the mouth or hands regularly until they become aware of when it is necessary to do this to maintain a pleasant appearance. The physiotherapist or speech therapist can be asked to recommend a routine to improve control of the muscles involved in swallowing and maintaining mouth closure. These actions can also be encouraged at mealtimes, morning or afternoon drinks sessions, and during tasting sessions.

Many children dislike, or resist, washing face and hands or cleaning teeth, but it is important for reasons of health and appearance that they should learn to carry out these activities or accept having them done for them. Children may resist because they have not been given a recognisable indication of what is going to happen; or they may be particularly sensitive to touch on hands or face. In order to help children to tolerate and ultimately to cooperate or take part in these processes, it is vital to prepare them for what is about to happen and to carry out the actions gently but firmly. Attention must be given to the temperature of water, the texture of the cloth or brush, and the vigour with which the procedure is carried out. Many children can be guided through the action required to squeeze a cloth and wash the face. Actions of this kind can help to increase self-awareness, particularly if there is a mirror available, as well as encouraging washing skills.

Within the classroom, mirror work can promote recognition of self and others, and identification of facial features, body parts, and clothing. It can encourage children to take an interest in their own appearance. Brushing and combing hair, and putting on hats, scarves, jewellery, spectacles, and so on can all be enhanced by the use of a mirror. Dressing up, either in a free situation or in guided singing or drama sessions, can also help to increase self-awareness and interest in personal appearance and grooming.

In schools which have bathing or showering facilities it is possible to include hair washing and bathing in the individual programmes for pupils who dislike and resist these activities at home. Gradually children can be helped to tolerate and cooperate with these procedures which can be of great assistance to their carers.

ENVIRONMENTAL CONTROL

This component sets out to develop children's ability to make decisions. This is fundamental to personal independence. Complete independence will be achieved only if children are able to make appropriate decisions and carry out the necessary actions to achieve the intended result. Complete dependence exists only if all decisions and all actions are carried out by others. A degree of independence is possible, therefore, even if children must rely on others to carry out the actions intended. It is all too easy to induce a greater degree of dependence than necessary by denying children the chance to make decisions or to carry out actions of which they are capable. This reduces the degree of control they can exercise over the environment and the experiences which arise from it.

There is always an element of decision-making in any intentional action, whether it is at a simple level of rejection or withdrawal *versus* acceptance, or at a complex level involving an independent course of action to achieve a predetermined goal. The context of decision-making can vary enormously in complexity and many cognitive elements are involved. It is important to promote children's ability to make choices and to take decisions which match their cognitive level. They should not be presented with choices which make too great a demand on their abilities as this is likely to reduce the possibility of a considered choice being made. Clearly children's degree of independence and environmental control will be closely associated with their achievements in the components of the cognitive curriculum.

If children are to be enabled to exercise the maximum degree of independence compatible with their disabilities, the curriculum must provide them with opportunities to make considered choices and decisions based on understanding of a given situation, and to acquire physical and communication skills to enable them to put their decisions into effect. This will allow them to exert some degree of control over their environment.

The simplest choice situation is one in which the option is either to do something or not to do it. Most children make the choice either to accept or refuse food or drink. Some children may choose either to cooperate or to resist in washing and dressing or some kind of classroom activity. The element of choice lies mainly in the nature of the children's response in a given context which they understand.

It is important, however, for children to be able to foresee events and choose between two alternatives. In order to encourage them to make a considered choice it may be necessary to identify one or two preferences, or even dislikes, which can be used as options. It may also be necessary to establish a consistent response which children can use to indicate choice, such as looking, reaching, using a gesture, or vocalising. To make choices at this level children must have some degree of attention control. They must also have acquired sufficient discrimination skills and concepts of causality and means-end relationships to be able to associate their responses in the choice situation with the result or object they desire.

More complex decision-making will involve choice situations with a larger number of options from which to choose, or a wider range of possible responses. This level of decision-making will involve greater discrimination skills, situational understanding, and an appreciation of the likely consequences of a particular response or course of action.

Decision-making can be incorporated into many activities. The most salient situations are likely initially to be those relating to personal needs, such as eating and drinking, toileting, maintaining a comfortable temperature, and the need for attention. Preferred objects, activities, and people can be used to introduce an element of choice into even the most structured routines. However, there will be more freedom to make decisions in less structured activities, such as exploratory play, drama games, and creative activities. These will allow children to generalise their decision-making skills in situations where both the result and the means of achieving it is under their control.

Conclusion

It is evident from this discussion of the core curriculum and its component areas that it is impossible to separate learning in one area from any of the other areas; to do so would only contribute to the fragmentation of learning and acquisition of splinter skills. The activities that have been suggested in the discussion of the component areas provide means of achieving the objectives and working towards the aims set in each area of the children's individual programmes. Although many of the same activities can be used in several different curriculum areas to work towards a variety of different objectives, it is important to select and plan them carefully to ensure that they are presented in ways which will facilitate learning that is relevant to the objectives which have been identified for individual children, at the same time reinforcing and enhancing learning in other areas.

Activities carried out in class will depend upon the agreed priorities of parents/carers and teachers when identifying aims and in setting objectives in relation to each child's needs and stage of development. They will also reflect the ingenuity and expertise of the teacher in devising appropriate activities and making good use of the facilities and resources within the school and the local community. Consequently curriculum activities will vary widely according to the needs of the individual children, the staff available, and the conditions in any given place and time.

References

MOVEMENT
Bower, T. G. R. *A Primer of Infant Development*. Oxford: W. H. Freeman, 1977.
Bruner, J. *Heinz Werner Lectures in Developmental Psychology*. Worcester, Mass: Clark University, 1968.
Cratty, B. J. *Perceptual and Motor Development in Infants and Children*. London: Prentice Hall Inc., 1979.
Held, R., Hein, A. Movement produced stimulation in the development of visually guided behaviour. *J. Comparative Physiol. & Psychol.*, 1963; **56**, 872-76.
Kephart, N. *The Slow Learner in the Classroom*. London: Charles E. Merrill Books Inc., 1960.
Ouvry, C. *Considerations in Planning the Curriculum for Profoundly Handicapped Children*. (Unpubl. thesis). London: Univ. London Inst. of Education, 1983.
Sherborne, V. The significance of early movement experiences in the development of severely retarded children. *In* Upton, G. (Ed.). *Physical and Creative Activities for the Mentally Handicapped*. Cambridge: Cambridge Univ. Press, 1979.

SENSORY AWARENESS
Bower, T. G. R. *A Primer of Infant Development*. Oxford: W. H. Freeman and Co., 1977.
McInnes, J. M., Treffrey, J. A. *Deaf-Blind Infants and Children*. Milton Keynes: Open Univ. Press, 1982.
Ouvry, C. *Considerations in Planning the Curriculum for the Profoundly Handicapped Child*. (Unpubl. thesis.) London: Univ. London Inst. of Educ., 1983.
Walker, M., Armfield, A. What is the Makaton Vocabulary? *Spec. Educ.: Forward Trends*, 1981; **8**:2, 19-20.

PERCEPTUAL MOTOR
Bower, T. G. R. *A Primer of Infant Development*. Oxford: W. H. Freeman, 1977.
Bruner, J. S. Organisation of early skilled action. *Child Devel.*, 1973; **44**, 1-11.
Bruner, J. S. *Beyond the Information Given*. London: Allen & Unwin, 1974.
Cratty, B. J. *Perceptual and Motor Development in Infants and Children*. Hemel Hempstead: Prentice Hall Inc., 1979.
Uzgiris, I. C. Ordinality in the development of schemas for relating to objects. *In* Hellmuth, J. (Ed.). *Exceptional Infant (Vol. 1)*. Seattle: Special Child Publications, 1967.

COGNITIVE
Bailey, I. J. *Structuring a Curriculum for Profoundly Mentally Handicapped Children*. Glasgow — Jordanhill Coll. of Educ., 1983.
Bower, T. G. R. *A Primer of Infant Development*. Oxford: W. H. Freeman, 1977.
Bruner, J. S. *Beyond the Information Given*. London: Allen & Unwin, 1974.

Cooper, J., Moodley, M., Reynell, J. *Helping Language Development*. London: Edward Arnold, 1978.

Ginsberg, H., Opper, S. *Piaget's Theory of Intellectual Development*. London: Prentice-Hall Inc., 1979.

Nelson, K. Infants' short-term progress towards one component of object permanence. *Merril-Palmer Quarterly*, Jan. 1974; **20**:1, 3-8.

Oates, J. (Ed.). *Early Cognitive Development*. London: Croom Helm, 1979.

Piaget, J. *The Construction of Reality in the Child*. (Trans. Cook, M.) London: Routledge & Kegan Paul, 1954.

Piaget, J. *The Origin of Intelligence in Children*. (Trans. Cook, M.) London: Routledge & Kegan Paul, 1953.

Rostron, A., Sewell, D. *Microtechnology in Special Education*. London: Croom Helm, 1984.

COMMUNICATION

Bluma, S., Shearer, M., Frohman, A., Hilliard, J. *Portage Guide to Early Education*. Windsor: NFER/Nelson, 1976.

Cooper, J., Moodley, M., Reynell, J. *Helping Language Development*. London: Edward Arnold, 1978.

Cunningham, C., Sloper, P. *Helping your Handicapped Baby*. London: Souvenir Press, 1978.

Deich, R., Hodges, P. M. *Language without Speech*. London: Souvenir Press, 1977.

Evans, P. L., Ware, J. *Special Care Provision: The Education of Children with Profound and Multiple Learning Difficulties*. Windsor: NFER/Nelson, 1987.

Gilham, B. *The First Words Language Programme*. London: Allen & Unwin, 1979.

Halliday, H. *Explorations in the Function of Language*. London: Arnold, 1973.

Jago, J. L., Jago, A. G., Hart, M. An evaluation of the total communication approach for teaching language skills to developmentally delayed pre-school children. *Educ. & Train. of the Ment. Retard.*, 1984; **19**:3, 175-182.

Jeffree, D., McConkey, R. *Let me Speak*. London: Souvenir Press, 1976.

Jones, P. R., Cregan, A. *Sign and Symbol Communication for Mentally Handicapped People*. London: Croom Helm, 1986.

Kiernan, C., Jordan, R., Saunders, C. *Starting Off*. London: Souvenir Press, 1978.

Kiernan, C., Reid, B., Jones, L. *Signs and Symbols: a review of literature and survey of use of non-vocal communication*. London: Heinemann Educational, 1982.

Kiernan, C., Reid, B. *Pre-verbal Communication Schedule*. Windsor: NFER/Nelson, 1986.

Locke, A. *Living Language*. Windsor: NFER/Nelson, 1985.

Masidlover, M., Knowles, W. *The Derbyshire Language Scheme*. (Private publication.) 1982. Avail. from: Psychological Service Education Office Grosvenor Rd, Ripley, Derbyshire.

Peter, M., Barnes, R. *Signs, Symbols and Schools*. Windsor: NFER, 1982.

Sherborne, V. The significance of early movement experiences in the development of severely retarded children. *In* Upton, G. (Ed.). *Physical and Creative Activities for the Mentally Handicapped*. Cambridge: Cambridge Univ. Press, 1979.

Simon, G. B. *The Next Step on the Ladder: assessment and management of children with multiple handicaps. (4th edn.)*. Kidderminster: BIMH Publications, 1986.

Tebbs, T. (Ed.). *Ways and Means*. Basingstoke: Globe Educational, 1978.

Walker, M., Armfield, A. What is the Makaton Vocabulary? *Spec. Educ.: Forward Trends*, 1981; **8**:2, 19-20.

Walker, M. The Makaton Vocabulary. *In* Tebbs, T. (Ed.). *Ways and Means*. Basingstoke: Globe Educational, 1978.

White, M., East, K. *The Wessex Revised Portage Language Checklist*. Windsor: NFER, 1984.

INDEPENDENCE

Anderson, C. *Feeding — a Guide to Assessment and Intervention with Handicapped Children*. Glasgow: Jordanhill Coll. of Educ., 1983.

Bailey, I. J. *Structuring a Curriculum for Profoundly Mentally Handicapped Children*. Glasgow: Jordanhill Coll. of Educ., 1983.

Cotton, E. *Conductive Education and Cerebral Palsy*. London: The Spastics Society, 1980.

Evans, P., Ware, J. *Special Care Provision: the Education of Children with Profound and Multiple Learning Difficulties*. Windsor: NFER/Nelson, 1987.

Ouvry, C. *Considerations in Planning the Curriculum for Profoundly Handicapped Children*. (Unpubl. thesis.) London: Univ. London Inst. of Educ., 1983.

Warner, J. *Helping Your Handicapped Child with Early Feeding*. Winslow: Winslow Press, 1981.

Further reading

MOVEMENT

Cottam, P., McCartney, E., Cullen, C. The effectiveness of conductive education principles with profoundly retarded multiply handicapped children. *Brit. J. Disord. Commun.*, 1985; **20**:1, 45-60.

Cottam, P., Sutton, A. *Conductive Education: a System for Overcoming Motor Disorder*. London: Croom Helm, 1986.

Cotton, E. *Conductive Education and Cerebral Palsy*. London: The Spastics Society, 1980.

Evans, J. Massage - an alternative starting point. *Sense*, 1986; **32**:1, 15.

Groves, L. (Ed.). *Physical Education for Special Needs*. Cambridge: Cambridge Univ. Press, 1979.

Holle, B. *Motor Development in Children - Normal and Retarded*. Oxford: Blackwell Scientific, 1976.

Hollis, K. *Progress to Improved Movement: for handicapped children and adults with poor posture*. Kidderminster: BIMH Publications, 1977.

Hollis, K. *Progress to Standing: for children with severe physical handicap*. Kidderminster: BIMH Publications, 1977.

Jennings, S. (Ed.). Creative Therapy. London, Pitman, 1975.

Kirby, M. *Sherborne and Movement: a Descriptive Study*. Bristol: Bristol Poly., 1984.

Knill, C., Knill, M. *Body Awareness, Contact and Communication*. Distr.: Wisbech, LDA.

Levitt, S. *Treatment of Cerebral Palsy and Motor Delay*. Oxford: Blackwell Scientific, 1982.

Scrutton, D. (Ed.). *Management of Motor Disorders of Children with Cerebral Palsy*. London: Spastics Internat. Med. Publ., 1984.

Upton, G. (Ed.). *Physical and Creative Activities for the Mentally Handicapped*. Cambridge: Cambridge Univ. Press, 1979.

SENSORY AWARENESS

Bower, T. G. R. *The Perceptual World of the Child*. London: Fontana, 1977.

Bradley, H., Snow, B. *Working with Mentally Handicapped Adults with Additional Visual and Hearing Impairments: a Guide for Carers*, 1986. Avail. from: SENSE, 4 Church Road, Edgbaston, Birmingham.

Byrne, D. J., Stevens, C. P. Mentally handicapped children's responses to vibro-tactile and other stimuli as evidence for the existence of a sensory heirarchy. *Apex, (now Ment. Hand.)* 1980; **8**:3, 96-98.

Byrne, D. J., Stevens C. P. *Use of Vibro-tactile Stimulation to Develop Skills with the Multiply Disabled Child.* London: Niagara Therapy UK Ltd., 1982.

Chapman, E. *Visually Handicapped Children and Young People.* London: Routledge & Kegan Paul, 1978.

Evans, J. Massage — an alternative starting point. *Sense*, 1986; **32**:1.

Freeman, P. *Understanding the Deaf-Blind Child.* London: Heinemann Medical Books, 1975.

Freeman, P. *The Deaf-Blind Baby.* London: Heinemann Medical Books, 1985.

Hogg, J., Sebba, J. *Profound Retardation and Multiple Impairment, Vol. 2. Education and Therapy*, London: Croom Helm, 1986.

Longhorn, F. *A Resource Bank for the Very Special Child.* Northampton: Wren Spinney School, 1985.

Kiernan, C., Jones, M. *The Behaviour Assessment Battery.* Windsor: NFER/Nelson, 1982.

Royal National Institute for the Blind. *Guidelines for Teachers and Parents of Visually Handicapped Children with Additional Handicaps.* London: RNIB (no date).

Wyman, R. *Multiply Handicapped Children.* London: Souvenir Press, 1986.

Periodicals

Information Exchange. Available from Royal National Institute for the Blind, 224 Great Portland Street, London W1N 6AA.

Talking Sense. Available from SENSE — The National Deaf-Blind and Rubella Assoc., 311 Gray's Inn Road, London, WC1X 8PT.

PERCEPTUAL MOTOR

Kiernan, C. *Starting Off.* London: Souvenir Press, 1978.

Kiernan, C. *Analysis of Programmes for Teaching.* Basingstoke: Globe Educational, 1981.

McInnes, J. A., Treffrey, J. M. *Deaf-blind Infants and Children.* Milton Keynes: Open Univ. Press, 1982.

Neilsen, L. *The Comprehending Hand.* (Trans. Robinson, A., 1979). From: Socialstyren, Kristineberg 6, Post box 2555, 2100 Copenhagen Ø.

COGNITIVE

Beurmann, M. M., Lahm, L. Babies and robots: technology to assist learning of young multiply disabled children. *Rehab. Literature*, 1984; **45**:7-8, 194-201.

Coupe, J., Levy, D. The object related scheme assessment procedure. *Ment. Hand.*, 1985; **13**:1, 22-24.

Coupe, J. Porter, J. *The Education of Children with Severe Learning Difficulties.* London: Croom Helm, 1986.

Cunningham, C., Sloper, P. *Helping your Handicapped Baby.* London: Souvenir Press, 1978.

Gardner, J. M., Murphy, J., Smith, J. M. Multiply handicapped children — an attempt to look at their education and to suggest a more structured approach. *Apex*, now *Ment. Hand.*, 1980; **8**:1, 6-8.

Hogg, J., Sebba, J. *Profound Retardation and Multiple Impairment Vol. 2: Education and Therapy.* London: Croom Helm, 1986.

Jeffree, D., McConkey, R., Hewson, S. *Let Me Play.* London: Souvenir Press, 1977.

Kiernan, C. *Analysis of Programmes for Teaching.* Basingstoke: Globe Educational, 1981.

Kiernan, C. *Starting Off.* London: Souvenir Press, 1978.

Kiernan, C., Jones, M. *Behaviour Assessment Battery.* Windsor: NFER/Nelson, 1977.

Ouvry, C. *Using Electronic Equipment in the Curriculum for Profoundly Multiply Handicapped Children.* (Unpubl.). Avail. from: BIMH Information/Resource Centre, Wolverhampton Road, Kidderminster, DY10 3PP.

Simon, G. B. *The Next Step on the Ladder: assessment and management of children with multiple handicaps.* (4th Edn.). Kidderminster, BIMH Publications, 1986.

Tait, J. A., Graham, G. V., Watts, G. T. *Computer Assisted Development with Profoundly Retarded Multiply Handicapped Children.* Avail. from: Hillside House, Kilton Hospital School, Worksop, Nottinghamshire.

Walsall Working Party on Curriculum Development for the Multiply Handicapped ESN(S) Child. *Teaching the Multiply Handicapped.* Walsall: Walsall Education Department, (OOP).

York, J., Nietupski, J., Hamre-Nietupski, S. A decision-making process for using micro switches. *J. Assoc. Persons with Severe Handicaps*, 1985; **10**:4, 214-223.

COMMUNICATION

Bruner, J. S. The ontogenesis of speech acts. *J. Child Lang.,* 1974; **2**:19, 1-20.

Cregan, A. *Sigsymbols: a graphic aid to communication and language development.* Paper delivered at a curriculum conference organised by Cambridge Inst. Educ., 1984.

Groves, L. *Physical Education in Special Needs.* Cambridge: Cambridge Univ. Press, 1979.

Halliday, H. *Learning How to Mean.* London: Edward Arnold, 1975.

Jones, K. R. A rebus system of non-fade visual language. *Child: Care, Health & Dev.*, 1979; **5**,1-7.

Kiernan, C., Reid, B., Jones, L. M. *Signs and Symbols: a review of literature and survey of use of non-vocal communication systems.* London: Heinemann Educational, 1982.

Leeming, K., Swann, W., Coupe, J., Mittler, P. *Teaching Language and Communication to the Mentally Handicapped (Schools Council Bulletin No. 8).* London: Evans/Methuen Educational, 1979.

McDonald, E. T. (Ed.). *Teaching and Using Blissymbolics.* Toronto: Blissymbolics Communications Institute, 1980. Avail. from: LDA/Living and Learning, Duke Street, Wisbech.

Minifie, M. K., Lloyd, L. L. (Eds.). *Communicative and Cognitive Abilities — Early Behavioral Assessment.* Baltimore: Univ. Park Press, 1978.

Schaffer, H. R. (Ed.). *Studies in Mother-Infant Interaction.* London: Academic Press Inc., 1977.

Schiefelbusch, R. L. (Ed.). *Non-speech Language and Communication - Analysis and Intervention.* Baltimore: University Park Press, 1980.

Smith, J. M., Murphy, J. W. Non-vocal communication with the multiply handicapped child. *Apex* (now *Ment. Hand.*), 1978; **6**:3, 16-17.

Snow, C. E. The development of conversation between mothers and babies. *J. Child Lang., 1976;* **4**:1, 1-11.

Stern, D. *The First Relationship: Infant and Mother.* London: Fontana, 1979.

CHAPTER 9

Implementing the curriculum

The unique and complex needs of the children in a special class makes implementation of a comprehensive individual programme for every child seem a daunting task. However, the individual programmes devised will include only those curriculum components which are particularly relevant to each child's current educational needs; and since many of the activities described contribute to components in different curriculum areas, a well-chosen activity, carefully planned, can in one session work towards several of the stated objectives at once. This applies whether the activity is carried out in a group or a one-to-one teaching situation.

Consideration must be given to the organisation of space, time, and staff, as well as to the activities that are selected in order to achieve efficient implementation of a balanced and comprehensive curriculum which caters for the needs of all the children.

Assessment of educational needs

Before any curriculum planning or classroom organisation can take place it is necessary for the teacher to have a general idea of the range of needs of the children in the class and, thus, the likely curriculum priorities. Chapter 7 described how to draw up an Initial Profile for each child and this may assist the teacher to gain an overview of class needs and to identify individual priorities which will guide the choice of activities included in the timetable.

Figure 11 (page 104) shows how the information provided by the Initial Profiles can be used in the curriculum model described to plan a timetable of activities which incorporates the needs of individual children and groups. The philosophy will establish the general aims and statement of intent for the clsss as a whole. The Initial Profiles will produce information in all four developmental areas for every child. Reference to the aims in these four areas will suggest specific long-term aims which will form the basis of the individual programmes. These specific aims will indicate the curriculum areas most likely to be relevant, and reference to these will guide the choice of components most appropriate for inclusion in individual programmes and the short-term aims within these components. The aims of the curriculum components will assist in formulating specific objectives in children's individual programmes and will help to determine the activities that will be used to work towards achieving them.

Group activities can be devised which will incorporate objectives that are relevant for all the children, even though different children may be working on different objectives within the same activity. Individual activities can be planned which will include the objectives that are specific to each child and which require a more intensive teaching approach. Using the curriculum model in this way helps to ensure that the range of activities is manageable, even when catering for each child's needs on an individual basis.

Timetabling

Organisation of time in a special class is dependent upon many factors: organisation of the school as a whole; the facilities available; the support of specialist teachers within the school; and the availability of peripatetic teachers and support staff from other services. Activities have to be fitted into a timetable which is determined, to some extent, by all these factors.

Certain fixed events occur, either daily, weekly, or at other regular intervals, such as arrival and departure times, mealtimes, breaktimes, and activities which involve the whole school, such as assembly. The teacher has little or no control over the timing of these events and all other activities have to be fitted in around them.

There are other fixed times which are determined by the school organisation, including the use of facilities such as the hall, specialist areas, and transport for off-site activities. The teacher is at liberty to decide how to use these facilities to the best advantage of the children in the class. The general nature of these activities will be predetermined, but their detailed planning and the number of children and staff who will be using the facilities at any given time will be decided by the teacher. Support from specialist teachers within the school, peripatetic teachers, and paramedical staff or volunteers is also likely to be available at fixed times. The teacher will have to negotiate the amount of time that can be allocated to the class and will be involved in joint planning of group and individual sessions with the appropriate personnel.

Some activities have to be undertaken regularly, possibly several times a day, such as toileting and other aspects of personal care. These must be timetabled appropriately to meet the needs of individual children. The teacher must guard against the routine dictating the needs of the children rather than reflecting their needs and stage of development. Other chores, which are particularly necessary in the special class, include washing, cleaning of equipment, and disposal of waste. There is no choice about whether or not to carry out these activities, but there may be a degree of flexibility as to their timing.

Having taken account of all these factors the teacher will timetable activities for the remaining periods on the basis of the children's individual needs. At this stage it will be necessary to decide whether the activities are best carried out as group or individual sessions. Such decisions depend in part on the availability and expertise of staff.

It is important for the teacher to ensure that all four developmental areas are incorporated in the timetabled activities for the children, at the same time making certain that the emphasis is in the areas of greatest need for each child. The teacher must also check that there is an overall balance in the timetable between group and individual sessions. It is easy to equate individual programmes with one-to-one teaching; and to overlook the fact that all activities undertaken form part of all the children's individual programmes (although the potential for learning will vary). This can result in an over-emphasis on behavioural objectives and individual teaching sessions, at the expense of experiential or expressive objectives, thus minimising opportunities to generalise or acquire new skills in structured group activities, and ignoring the potential for learning which exists in every situation, even though it may not strictly be an "educational" activity. There are some objectives, particularly in the area of social and personal development, which are impossible to achieve in intensive, one-to-one teaching situations.

Organisation of space

Special classes vary enormously in the amount of space they have available and the number of children who must share it. Space is one of the greatest assets, particularly for children with profound handicaps who are likely to need floor activities, or to be positioned in equipment such as side lyers, standing frames, or special chairs which take up a great deal of room.

It is important for the teacher to plan the use of the classroom so that various activities can be carried out with a minimum amount of movement of furniture and equipment. If there is enough space, creating "zones" within the classroom for various types of activities may be the most convenient method of organisation. It is useful first to consider the main routes which link up the structural features, such as doorways, toilet area, storage space, and sink. The zones can then be planned so that these routes are not obstructed and free movement is facilitated. Other considerations in planning zones will include the source of light, so that highly visual activities can take place in an area where the light level can be controlled, and the location of power points, which will determine where activities involving the use of electrical equipment, can be organised.

One area of the room may be designated an interest area, where children can explore and occupy themselves with a minimum of adult intervention. An area for floor work, whether for individual exercises or group movement sessions, will almost certainly be needed. However, it is often neither convenient nor desirable to have large areas of floor space permanently filled with mats. It is preferable to put these down only when they are needed for group work. There can be no temptation then to leave children lying around on mats when they should be in more functional positions from which they can interact with their surroundings, or which are beneficial to their physical well-being.

An area for tables and appropriate seating is always necessary since, for most children, sitting is the best learning position and is essential for participating in many classroom activities, whether group or individual.

Where space allows a teaching area, in which the level of distraction and likelihood of interruption is less than in the rest of the classroom, can be set aside for intensive teaching on a one-to-one or small group basis. Ideally this will be a separate room, or even a converted cupboard, but failing this an area may have to be created in a corner of the classroom, perhaps shielded by screens, or divided from the main part of the room with storage units.

Equipment should be stored as near as possible to the area in which it is most frequently used. It can include large items and furniture, special aids, and collections of teaching materials. Many of the children will be using similar materials and equipment in their individual sessions, so resource boxes which contain all the necessary items for a given activity can be very useful. Resource boxes for specific activities such as basic skills, imitation, auditory training, tactile work, body image, early language, and many others can be created. Longhorn (1985) describes the Sensory Bank, which is a similar system used in her own school. A system where individual children have their own boxes or trays of items is less satisfactory, requiring duplication of equipment and materials, which are often both large and costly, and more time to maintain in good order.

Organisation of staff

The 12-school survey (Ouvry, 1983) shows that the size of special classes varies widely. In the schools surveyed the smallest class had five children and the largest 14. The number of staff also varies, but it is likely that each special class will have at least one class teacher and between two and five assistants depending upon the number of children in the class and the way staff are deployed throughout the school.

If there are many staff, communication can become a problem. It is vital that all members of staff know their own role and have access to daily plans to which they can refer. A regular time should be set aside every week when staff can meet to discuss any problems and exchange information. It is usually impossible for all members of the school team, including the various other professionals as well as teaching staff, to meet outside teaching hours. The benefits, in terms of more efficient organisation and increased expertise and enthusiasm, justify the use of a short period during the school day for such meetings. The insight of all members of the team is likely to be increased by the opportunity to contribute to the planning and organisation of the special class and also by occasional discussions on specific topics led by the class teacher, or an expert in the particular area being discussed. At these times the children will be supervised, but will be allowed to occupy themselves without intervention except in emergencies.

The class teacher, as well as organising the activities of the permanent classroom staff, must decide the most effective way of using the expertise of staff and, possibly peripatetic teachers who visit the school at various times during the week. There are several different models of classroom management which can be followed:

THE KEY WORKER

In this model each member of staff is allocated a number of children and is responsible for carrying out their individual programmes. The advantage of this system is that the adults get to know their own pupils very well and so become able to interpret their responses and work out strategies which are successful in eliciting desired responses. The class teacher remains responsible for identifying objectives and devising activities for the children but the key worker monitors their progress and discusses developments with the teacher. A sensitive and experienced key worker will make suggestions to the teacher and will be able to work towards objectives in a flexible and creative way.

ROOM MANAGEMENT

This system (Porterfield, Blunden, and Blewett, 1977) was devised to ensure maximum staff/client involvement in large institutions. It is particularly useful when there is an unfavourable staff/client ratio. In schools emphasis is upon each member of staff having a well defined role within the classroom. An individual worker takes children for short, one-to-one teaching sessions, whilst another member of staff ensures that the other children are engaged in appropriate activities and a third ensures that work in the classroom is maintained without interruptions or delay. If there are only two members of staff the last two roles can be combined. Where there are more than three members of staff there can be two or more individual workers.

SMALL GROUPS

In this form of organisation the class is split up into small groups. One or two members of staff are responsible for each group of children. There are several variations of this type of organisation and there is some evidence that, with carefully planned activities, children can learn as effectively in small groups as in one-to-one situations and that the amount of time in teaching situations is significantly increased (Coupe and Porter, 1986). Small group teaching can continue throughout the day, or it can be used for certain activities which are particularly suited to small group work.

AREA SPECIALISTS

In this system certain members of staff are responsible for activities in one particular curriculum area. Specialist teachers and support staff naturally work in this way, but when members of the classroom staff have specific skills and interests it is appropriate for them to use these in activities with the children. This is particularly useful in activities which require a special talent which is not shared by all, such as music, but it can also be used to increase expertise in certain areas. Although it is possible, it is not usual for this form of organisation to be employed throughout the day. It can combine particularly well with the small group system.

None of these forms of organisation is mutually exclusive. It is likely that the system used will change from time to time during the day, as different activities require different forms of organisation to be most effective. As the leader of a multidisciplinary team the class teacher needs a very clear idea of the aims of education for children with profound handicaps and of how all available personnel can contribute to the individual aims for every child. The teacher must recognise and value the expertise and skills of all members of the team, and must engage team members in all stages of educational planning in order to ensure the most effective use of their skills in the activities of the classroom.

A large number of staff and children involves complex planning, but it makes it possible to offer a wide range of activities at levels appropriate to the pupils. It is more difficult, in a small class with two or three members of staff, particularly if the children have very different needs, to offer both individual and group activities at appropriate levels. In this situation a policy of integration within the school as a whole is vital to ensure access to a wider curriculum for children based in the special class. It is important (see Part 1, Chapter 4) to remember that integration is not necessarily a one way process, however, and it does not have to be full time. It can be arranged on a sessional basis for individual pupils or for groups. This means that members of regular classes can join sessions in the special class as well as *vice versa*.

Carrying through a scheme of integration puts additional pressure on staff resources and the needs of all of the children must be carefully balanced. A well planned and supported scheme, however, can allow children the opportunity to experience a wider range of activities at appropriate levels.

Presentation of activities

Once the timetable has been decided, the activities devised, the equipment and materials assembled, and the staff deployed, the way in which tasks and activities are presented must be considered. There are certain general points, such as positioning, equipment and materials, and teaching techniques, which must be defined.

POSITIONING

The position of the children in relation to the adult must be considered and it must be decided whether teaching is likely to be most effective as an individual or group activity.

If it is a group activity, should the children be in chairs or sitting on the floor? Should they sit around a table or other equipment? Should they be close together or well spaced out? Can they be positioned at much the same level? Is the focus of attention (whether this is the adult, a piece of equipment, or the other members of the group) unobstructed? Is the expected action within the capability of every member of the group? Can the adult remain in one position and maintain the attention of the group, or will it be necessary to move from pupil to pupil to do so?

If it is an individual teaching session, does the child need to be face to face with the adult to maintain attention and carry out the task, or will teaching from the side or behind the child be more effective? (This may be necessary if obsessive fixation on the adult's face prevents the child from interacting with anything else in the surroundings and thus creates a barrier to learning.) Does the working position of the child make it necessary to place materials in unusual ways — on inclined tables, attached to or suspended over a child, on the floor, or at a very precise level — so that they are within the child's range of operation? Does equipment need to be fixed with clamps or other devices so that it remains within reach? If the child has severely restricted movement or a sensory loss are the materials placed within that child's range of action and perception, and in the optimum lighting conditions?

EQUIPMENT AND MATERIALS

Similar consideration must be given to the equipment or materials needed to carry out an activity. What are the physical properties of the objects such as size, shape, intensity of colour, or sound? What is their meaning for the children? Should the same materials be used every time, or should there be variety? If some change is to be made, what should it be and how often should it happen? (It is important that activities should become neither sterile and meaningless through lack of variety nor arbitrary and haphazard, and therefore equally meaningless, because of lack of consistency.)

There is much discussion at present about provision of age appropriate materials and activities for older pupils. This issue is very important as it reflects and influences the attitudes held towards people with profound handicaps generally. Their dignity is not enhanced by living or working in surroundings full of cuddly toys and *Disneyland* characters, or using equipment which is plainly produced for infants and young children. The problem is, how can provision be made which is both age and stage appropriate? Some changes are easy to make, for example traditional songs or pop music can be used to replace nursery rhymes. It is more difficult to provide age appropriate equipment which fulfils the same purpose as a toy produced for young children. There are now several suppliers of materials and equipment specially designed for use by people with profound handicaps which combine the simple characteristics necessary for learning at an appropriate level, with more adult designs and materials (see Appendix 4). Home-made equipment for specific purposes or for use by individual pupils is also less likely to look childish. Sports equipment, tape recorders and computers, simple musical instruments, and natural materials can be used appropriately by all age groups. There are certain activities, however, which are very difficult to teach using more adult equipment and materials. In these circumstances a degree of compromise may have to be accepted, and stage may have to take precedence over age appropriateness. Teachers must always be alert to the issue, however, and must make every effort to use materials and activities which fulfil both criteria.

TEACHING TECHNIQUES

The techniques and methods used by the teacher to elicit responses and encourage learning must be carefully chosen and implemented. There are many sources of information on learning theories and teaching techniques which can be effective in promoting learning in children with profound handicaps (Devereux, 1982; Child, 1981; Bailey, 1983; Hogg and Sebba, 1986). The teacher must consider whether free exploration, trial and error, modelling and imitation, shaping, backward and forward chaining, or a combination of some of these will be the most effective routes to learning in any given activity. Will rewards be effective? If so, what kind, how often, and how much? How can children's responses be maintained while reinforcements are faded? How can opportunities for generalisation of skills be provided?

Whatever method is chosen consistency in approach is vital for children with profound handicaps. All aspects of presentation must, therefore, be clearly stated so that everyone involved can apply the same techniques consistently in order to provide the greatest possible opportunity for learning to occur.

Monitoring of progress

Monitoring of individual programmes is an essential part of the teaching process in order to ensure that activities are appropriate for the children and that progress is being made towards achieving the set objectives. The variety of activities used within the curriculum call for different means of recording progress. Recording sheets, therefore, must be as flexible as possible in order to keep down the number of different kinds of forms needed.

Figure 14 is an example of a form of recording sheet which can be used to define not only the activity but context variables, such as the position of the child and adult, other relevant features of the learning environment, and the use of incentives. This Activity Record can be used to record a child's performance in a variety of different situations and to build up a profile of the repertoire of behaviours used by the child. Alternatively, it can be used to define the conditions for a series of structured sessions in conjunction with a detailed Response Record such as that shown in Figure 15 (page 178). A new activity would be required only if some change in the conditions were considered desirable.

Detailed records of specific responses in every teaching session may be necessary in certain activities, either to establish a child's baseline of response or to ascertain whether a skill is emerging or has reached the criterion set in the objective. This detailed recording is particularly important where inconsistency of response and performance, which may vary from day to day, makes it very difficult to evaluate progress. The Response Record enables details of a child's specific responses to objects, materials, or activities presented by the adult to be recorded on a form of grid. There is space for recording several trials each of a number of different ways of presentation of a variety of items; and the space left for

Name:	Alison Green	
Activity:	Sound localisation	
Objects and materials:	Four items from: Drum, Bells, Jingles	Loud Rattle, Soft Rattle, Crisp Bag, Whisper (name)

	Standing:	
Position of child and equipment used:	Sitting: Work chair/adjustable table	
	Kneeling:	
	Prone:	
	Supine:	

	Facing:	
Adult's position:	Behind: Standing and moving	
	Side — R: ,,	
	— L: ,,	

Proximity:	Within arm's length: Sounds at 9" and 18" from head	
	Beyond arm's length:	

Other variables: Screen between table and window to reduce distraction

Incentives/rewards: Play with toy when located correctly

Response or performance: Locate source of sound by turning head

Physical prompt by turning head gently

FIGURE 14. Activity record

Adapted from Leeming, Swann, Coupe, and Mittler (1979)

Name:	Alison Green			Activity:	Sound		Localisation	
Presentation:	Centre			Right			Left	Comments:
Trials:	1	2	3	1	2	3	1	2	3	
Items: 29/5/86 Drum	✓	✓	✓	✓	✓	✓	—	✗	✓	
Bells	✓	✓	✓	—	—	P	—	—	P	
L. Rattle	✓	✓	✓	—	✓	✓	—	—	P	
Crisp Bag	✓	✓	✓	✓	✓	✓	✗	✓	✓	

Key: ✓ = correct   x = incorrect   — = no response   p = prompt (specify)

FIGURE 15. Response record

comments can be used to make general observations on the session, such as the child's mood, cooperativeness, and any other relevant variables, or to refer to specific items used in the activity and note distractions, preferences, or suggested changes for the next session. The grid can be used for many activities, such as attention training, sound localisation, or object identification, and the results of several sessions can be shown on one sheet, depending upon the number of items included in each session.

Recording sheets help to minimise the amount of writing needed to describe progress and standardise the recording method. When "on the spot" recording is undertaken it is important to have a system which provides information in as clear a form as possible, using a code which is quick to use and easy to interpret. Without this, more time can be spent in recording than in working with the child, and the rhythm of the activity is constantly interrupted. Even so, in some instances it is necessary for one adult to work with the child and a second to record responses in order to avoid either missing crucial actions or disrupting the activity.

Very stringent criteria may have to be met before a skill is accepted as being well established. In a choice situation between two responses, a 50 per cent correct response would be expected by chance alone; but unless careful records are kept, this level of success could give the impression that the skill was fairly well established. Intuitive evaluations of a child's level of operating should never be discounted out of hand, particularly in terms of situational understanding and comprehension, but it is important to verify these assumptions wherever possible by systematic observation and recording in carefully structured situations.

For many activities it is an unnecessary waste of time to keep records in such detail. Even in one-to-one teaching of specific skills, once a child is beginning to respond consistently it is probably sufficient to record responses periodically rather than in every session. The same method of recording can be used on a weekly or a monthly time-scale to highlight cumulative changes whilst avoiding an unnecessary volume of paper-work. Subsequent transfer of results from the recording sheets onto a graph will show any trends or consistent changes in response.

For some activities, particularly those which use expressive objectives, the method of recording needed is less rigorous than described above and may take the form of written comments based upon informal observations made during sessions over a period of time (see Figure 16, page 180). Half termly or termly monitoring of a child's level of participation is probably adequate.

Whatever form of monitoring is chosen, it is vital that all aspects of every child's individual programme are reviewed regularly so that amendments and modifications can be made to accommodate the child's changing educational needs.

The learning environment

It is particularly important when working with children with profound handicaps for the teacher to consider the features of the learning environment in terms of the children's viewpoint.

NAME:		
Date:	**Activity/materials**	**Comments**
29/5/86	Tactile awareness: Shaking arms, hands & fingers with hands fur dry sand netting wood shavings	Relaxed when using hands, fur, sand — withdrew initially on contact with netting and shavings. Explored fur + sand by rubbing with both hands after physical prompt.

FIGURE 16. Record of informal observation of responses

Sometimes, mistakenly, a highly stimulating environment is created, with displays, mobiles, or constant background sound, which can have an adverse effect upon children with perceptual difficulties and problems in understanding their surroundings.

Sandhu and Hendriks-Jansen (1976) describe the features which their research has shown to be important in enabling children to interpret their surroundings. In particular they stress the importance of simplifying the visual impact and of accentuating the structural features such as doorways, corners, and large furniture or fixtures which lend definition to the environment and can become landmarks for children. The careful use of colour and pattern can help children to focus their attention and engage in visual exploration to discover features which have meaning for them. Textured or resonant surfaces can help them use alternative senses to orientate themselves within familiar environments.

Lighting is one of the most important aspects of the environment. Lighting conditions in different parts of the classroom tend to vary according to the source and intensity of the light. In some classrooms it is difficult to position children in even lighting and to avoid strong sources of light which shine directly at them or cause pools of light and shadow. Ideally there should be an area available where the level and direction of light can be easily controlled. This might be a corner of the classroom or a converted cupboard in which subdued lighting or highly focused areas of illumination, provided by table lamps or ultraviolet lights, can be installed. This will intensify the visual characteristics of the objects and materials being used and thus help to focus the children's attention on them and promote interaction. Good lighting conditions are particularly important when working with children who have visual deficits, but lighting has also been found to be effective in focusing the attention and promoting the exploratory behaviour of fully sighted pupils.

A distraction free teaching area may be necessary to enable some children to acquire new skills; but ultimately these skills must be generalised so that they can be carried out in more normal conditions. Even so, it is important that the demands upon children with profound handicaps are not made too great by unnecessary distractions, such as noises outside the classroom, interruptions, conversations between members of staff at inappropriate times, or noisy movement around the classroom; or other sources of confusion, such as elaborate displays, badly stored materials or equipment, or disorderly furniture which clutters the environment and adds to the perceptual difficulties of the pupils. Sometimes the source of these problems can be controlled by reorganising the use of time or space, but the teacher may have to resort to using curtains, screens, additional lighting, or new storage systems to reduce the complexity of the surroundings and create a good learning environment.

Since handicap has been described as dynamic, and relative to the expectations of others and the social contexts to which individuals are subject (Fish, 1985), the implication is that education should be informed not only by examining and changing children's behaviour in relation to the environment, but also by examining and if possible changing the environment if this is contributing to the degree of handicap experienced by the children.

◄──────────────── PARENTS/CARERS ────────────────►

EDUCATION	HEALTH	SOCIAL
IN SCHOOL.		
Daily Class teacher Classroom assistants	School nurse	
Sessional Specialist teachers Other class teachers and assistants Music therapist	Physiotherapist Occupational therapist Speech therapist	
Occasional Advisory teachers Educational psychologist Peripatetic teachers	Doctor Nurse Health visitor Dentist Dental nurse	Social worker
OUT OF SCHOOL:		
Home liaison teacher Class teacher (home visits) Child development team Staff of residential accommodation Nursing and/or care staff	Consultants: Paediatrician Psychologist Psychiatrist	Social worker Workers for voluntary bodies

FIGURE 17. Individuals likely to be involved with children attending the special class

Liaison with parents

It is important for the teacher to keep in close contact with the children's parents or carers, who must have the opportunity to be involved in all stages of planning and implementing the children's individual programmes. Parents' and carers' wishes must be taken into account when deciding on aims, and the children's programmes should be discussed with them. Some parents may wish to continue the programmes at home or to come into school to work with their children. Even if they do not, they must be kept informed of progress and of the children's activities during the week. A home/ school book in which parents/carers and school staff can write messages, which is sent to and from school with the respective child, is the most usual means of keeping in touch informally. It provides a simple method for regular exchange of information.

Figure 17 lists many of the people who might be involved with the special class as a whole and with individual pupils, both within and outside of the school. Coordination of services and integration of therapy, care, and education, with regular liaison with parents or carers to keep them fully informed, can be extremely complex. The amount of planning and liaison with other people to ensure the well-being of the pupils and effective implementation of a comprehensive curriculum in a class for children with profound handicaps should not be underestimated. It is essential for the teacher to have clear aims to give direction and a clear structure for the curriculum upon which to base the planning and organisation of the special class and so avoid confusion and fragmentation of provision.

References

Bailey, I. J. *Structuring a Curriculum for Profoundly Mentally Handicapped Children*. Glasgow: Jordanhill Coll. of Educ., 1983.

Child, D. *Psychology and the Teacher*. Eastbourne: Holt-Saunders, 1981.

Coupe, J., Porter, J. *The Education of Children with Severe Learning Difficulties*. London: Croom Helm, 1986.

Devereux, K. *Understanding Learning Difficulties*. Milton Keynes: Open Univ. Press, 1982.

Fish Report. *Educational Opportunities for All? Report of the Committee Reviewing Provision to Meet Special Educational Needs*. London: ILEA, 1985.

Hogg, J., Sebba, J. *Profound Retardation and Multiple Impairment Vol. 2 Education and Therapy*. London: Croom Helm, 1986.

Longhorn, F. *A Resource Bank for the Very Special Child*. Northampton: Wren Spinney School, 1985.

McBrien, J., Weightman, J. The Effect of a Room Management Procedure on the

Engagement of Profoundly Retarded Children. *Br. J. Ment. Subnorm*, 1980; **50**, 38-46.

Ouvry, C. *Considerations in Planning the Curriculum for the Profoundly Handicapped Child.* (Unpubl. thesis.) London: Univ. London Inst. of Educ., 1983.

Porterfield, J., Blunden, R. *Establishing Activity Periods in Special Needs Rooms with Adult Training Centres: Research Report No. 7.* Cardiff: Mental Handicap in Wales — Applied Research Unit, 1977.

Porterfield, J., Blunden, R., Blewitt, E. *Improving Environments for Profoundly Handicapped Adults: establishing staff routines for high client engagement.* Cardiff: Mental Handicap in Wales — Applied Research Unit, 1977.

Sandhu, J. Hendriks-Jansen, H. *Environmental Design for Handicapped Children.* Farnborough: Saxon House, 1976.

CHAPTER 10

Conclusion

This book has looked at the prevalence and definition of profound handicap, the criteria for placement in a special class, and the educational problems and barriers to learning that profound handicap can create. It has examined the management implications faced in school and various methods and benefits of integration of children with profound handicaps. It has also considered issues which are important in the planning and implementation of a balanced and integrated curriculum.

However, a study of the theory and practice of the education of children with profound handicaps would be incomplete without some mention of the nature of post-school provision. In the 12-school survey (Ouvry, 1983) all the schools were able to keep their pupils until the age of 19 years; indeed, several schools had pupils who were well over this age because of a lack of provision for school leavers with profound handicaps in the area. The facilities and support available for these young people after school leaving age are usually far less generous than those provided through the education service during school years. After school most places at day and residential centres for people with profound handicaps are provided by social services; some local health authorities also make provision in day care centres or residential establishments of various kinds. In a few areas independent organisations, such as national charities, also offer provision.

The interim report of the Mencap survey in the Manchester area (Hogg, Lambe, Cowie, and Coxon, 1987) found that 35 per cent of children still at school had a definite day care placement planned. Just over half of these were in an adult training centre or social education centre. The authors conclude that: "although three quarters of the parents who have found post-school placements are satisfied, the others see a need for improved therapeutic services in the centres, accompanied by provision that is more relevant to their sons and daughters with multiple handicaps". The survey carried out in South East England in 33 schools which offer places up to the age of 19 (Evans and Ware, 1987) shows that problems with post-school provision were reported in 36.4 per cent of the schools.

Even if there is a suitable form of provision in an area, there is still a general shortage of places and very rarely any choice of placement. The aims in different establishments vary widely and may differ fundamentally from those held by the schools that the young people previously attended. The régimes followed will inevitably reflect these aims.

It is now common practice in the final year at school for links to be made with the establishments to which school leavers will be transferring. This may be done through regular weekly courses, or by means of more informal visits of staff and pupils. It is important for the children to be prepared for the transfer, and equally important for school staff to know the form of provision which will be available. Skills which are likely to be most useful to individual pupils can then be incorporated into their school programmes to help prepare them for their new environment and routine, and the link visits will help to familiarise them further with the new routines and how to use their skills appropriately in the new setting. Forming links of this kind involves liaison with staff of the establishments concerned, and careful organisation of school staff and activities to enable the links to be maintained.

Clearly, teachers in charge of special classes face an extremely complex task which is both intellectually and physically demanding. It requires them to have well developed organisational and social skills in order to carry out the role of coordinator of a multi-disciplinary team in school and to be able to establish and maintain links with individuals, organisations, and establishments which are concerned with members of the special class outside of and after school. If teachers are to meet all these demands successfully, for the lasting benefit of children and young people with profound handicaps, it is essential that they be given adequate support in terms of staffing, advisors, facilities, and resources.

References

Evans, P., Ware, J. *Special Care Provision: the Education of Children with Profound and Multiple Learning Difficulties*. Windsor: NFER-Nelson, 1987.

Hogg, J., Lambe, L., Cowie, J., Coxon, J. *People with Profound Retardation and Multiple Handicaps Attending Schools or Social Education Centres*. London: Mencap, 1987.

Ouvry, C. *Considerations in Planning the Curriculum for the Profoundly Handicapped Child*. (Unpubl. thesis.) London: Univ. London Institute of Education, 1983.

INITIAL PROFILE

Name: ....Date of Birth:................................

Address: ....Telephone:................................

Medical condition: ....

....

Medication: ....

Hospital or GP: ....

Other professionals involved: ....

....

....

The Initial Profile is not intended to be an exhaustive checklist but a guide for use when constructing an overall profile of the abilities and difficulties of a child with profound handicaps. The questions are intended to direct the teacher's observations towards points which will form a basis for first decisions on priority areas in the educational programme and personal management of the pupil. The Profile will also indicate areas in which further detailed observations and assessments will be needed before realistic objectives can be set, and the other professionals who need to be involved.

The Initial Profile is divided into four sections, as follows:

Section 1. Physical development
Section 2. Perceptual development
Section 3. Intellectual development
Section 4. Personal/social development.

These Sections correspond with the four major developmental areas of the curriculum and all must be completed to give an overall picture of the child's current level of function.

SECTION 1. Physical Development

Comments

1. Voluntary movement

RESTRICTIONS

Is there any medical condition, eg, brittle bones, dislocations, heart condition, which restricts the movements of the child?

Is there any deformity, eg, contractures, malformation of bones, which restricts the movements possible (whether active or passive)?

Is there any significant disturbance of muscle tone, eg, spasticity, hypotonia, which affects the range of movements possible?

RANGE

Is the full range of movement possible?

If the range is restricted, to what extent and for what reason?

Is the full range available used actively by the child or is passive movement necessary?

CONTROL

Are early reflexes, eg, startle reflex, tonic neck reflex, stepping reflex, still present?

Are movements involuntary and random, or are they under voluntary control and intentional?

Are movements goal directed?

If movements are goal directed are they accurate and well controlled, or laborious and imprecise?

Do other limbs move unnecessarily when required movements are being made?

Comments

Are other limbs used in a complementary way, eg, holding objects in place with one hand while operating with the other?

2. Development

Are the patterns of motor development: normal for the child's age, normal but delayed, or abnormal?

3. Sitting/standing posture

To maintain a *safe* and *functional* position how much support is necessary when:

SITTING

Can the child sit unsupported on a chair?

Can the child sit unsupported on the floor?

Is there a particular way, eg, cross legged, long sitting, the child should sit?

When sitting does the child need the support of a special chair?

When sitting does the child need support, eg, at hips, chest, head, legs, knees, feet?

When sitting does the child need safety straps, eg, full harness, or lap, groin, chest, or foot straps?

STANDING

Can the child support own weight through the legs?

Can the child stand independently?

Can the child stand using furniture for support?

Can the child stand when assisted by another person?

If the child can stand with assistance, how much support is necessary?

Comments

Can the child regain balance?

Does the child use a standing frame for support, eg, at hips, chest, knees, or with foot straps?

Does the child use a standing box?

4. Mobility and locomotion

Can the child move around:

UNASSISTED

Can the child walk normally?

Can the child use supports in the surroundings, eg, furniture, rails, to move around?

Does the child move around by crawling/creeping?

Does the child move around by bottom shuffling?

Does the child move around by rolling?

ASSISTED

Does the child walk with a walking aid, eg, frame, rollator?

Does the child walk with adult support?

If adult support is needed how is it given?

RANGE

How far can the child move independently?

How far can the child move with assistance?

Does the child move around actively in the environment?

Does the child need encouragement or prompting to move around?

5. Positioning

Which positions are beneficial for physical development and prevention of deformity?

Is any equipment necessary to maintain a good position?

Comments

What type and angle of seating is needed?

If using a side lyer, which side should the child lie on?

If using a side lyer, how much support is necessary?

If using a wedge, what size is required?

If using a wedge, how much support is necessary?

What type of standing frame is needed?

Which positions are functional and encourage or enable the child to explore the surroundings?

6. **Hand use**

Is there any position in which the child habitually holds the hands?

AWARENESS

Does the child watch one or both hands moving in front of the face?

Does the child suck thumb or fingers of either hand?

Does the child touch own body parts with the hands?

Are any of these actions self-stimulatory or self-injurious?

Does the child bring both hands together in the midline?

CONTACT WITH THE SURROUNDINGS

Does the child swipe at, or reach towards, objects?

Does the child touch or finger surfaces?

Does the child hold objects?

Does the child pass objects from one hand to the other?

GRASP

Does the child show grasp reflex when an object is placed in the hand?

Does the child use a flat palmar grasp (fingers flat to palm of hand)?

Does the child use scissor grasp (between side of thumb and index finger)?

Does the child use pincer grip (tips of thumb and fingers)?

Does the child open hands voluntarily to grasp objects?

Does the child open hands voluntarily to release objects?

Does the child show any preference for using either hand?

7. **Obstructions to learning**

Does the child have to rely upon others to carry out actions?

Is the child unwilling or reluctant to carry out movements of which s/he is capable?

Does the child resist or withdraw when being moved?

8. **Detailed assessment**

Does the child need in depth assessment by a physiotherapist or an occupational therapist?

Comments

SECTION 2. Perceptual Development

	Comments
1. Awareness and acuity	

Has the child any apparent (or known) defect of hearing?

Has the child any apparent (or known) defect of vision?

Has the child any other sensory handicap?

Does the child respond to touch stimuli?

Does the child respond to visual stimuli?

Does the child respond to sound stimuli?

Does the child respond to smell or taste stimuli?

Does the child show a startle response as a reaction to change (stimulus) in the immediate surroundings?

Does the child still in response to change (stimulus) in the immediate surroundings?

Does the child show excitement in response to change (stimulus) in the immediate surroundings?

Does the child search for/locate change (stimulus) in the immediate surroundings?
How intense must a stimulus be to produce a response?

Does the child show awareness of similar changes (stimuli) at a distance?

2. Selective attention/discrimination

Does the child respond more frequently or consistently to some stimuli than to others? If so, specify touch, visual, sound, smell, taste.

Comments

Does the child habitually ignore some stimuli? If so, specify touch, visual, sound, smell, taste.

Does the child habitually respond to new stimuli?

Does the child habitually respond to familiar stimuli?

Does the child show preference for or dislike of certain things? If so, specify.

3. Consistency and differentiation of response

Does the child respond consistently and in the same way to change, or is the response variable in frequency and type?

Does the child respond in the same way to all stimuli, or does the response change according to the properties of the stimulus?

4. Concentration/distractibility

Is the child's attention easily distracted by events in the surroundings?

Can the child concentrate on an activity long enough to achieve a goal?

Does the child constantly have to be "brought back" on task?

Does the child perseverate and ignore all other stimuli or events?

Is it difficult to attract the child's attention?

5. Obstructions to learning

What prevents the child from acquiring information from the surroundings?

What prevents the child from responding in appropriate ways?

	Comments
6. Detailed assessment In which areas is a further detailed assessment necessary? Which other professionals need to be involved in this assessment?	

SECTION 3. Intellectual Development

	Comments
1. Attention control Does the child attend to people/objects which are nearby? Does the child follow the direction of attention of other people? Can the child transfer attention from one object/person to another and back to the first again? **2. Environmental understanding** Does the child show any recognition or anticipation of daily routines? Does the child show any recognition of specific people, objects, sounds or events? **3. Exploratory behaviour** Does the child actively explore objects? Does the child actively explore the immediate surroundings? Does the child use a range of actions, eg, shake, bang, push, pull, drop, finger, when exploring objects?	

Comments

Does the child do the same thing with every object, or use different actions with different objects?

4. Use of objects

Does the child put things in and out of containers?

Does the child use two objects together deliberately?

Does the child use objects purposefully to achieve a result?

Does the child use objects appropriately?

5. Early concepts

Does the child look for objects which have disappeared?

Does the child expect objects to reappear (object permanence)?

Does the child expect to find objects in their usual place?

Does the child associate actions with results (cause and effect)?

Does the child use objects purposefully to achieve a result (means-end relationship)?

Does the child use objects effectively, get round obstacles, correct mistakes (problem solving)? If so, specify.

Does the child match objects by attributes, eg, function, colour, shape?

Does the child sort collections of objects using own categories?

Does the child sort collections of objects using another person's categories?

	Comments
6. Understanding of symbols	
Does the child identify miniature objects with their use?	
Does the child associate realistic pictures and photographs with objects?	
Does the child carry out "pretend" play?	
Does the child identify line drawings of objects?	
Does the child understand any words?	
Does the child use any words?	
Does the child understand any gestures or signs?	
Does the child use any gestures or signs?	
Does the child use a two-dimensional system, eg, *Blissymbolics, Rebus, Sig-symbols, Makaton symbols?*	
7. Obstructions to learning	
What is likely to cause the child major difficulties in learning skills and understanding experiences?	
8. Detailed assessment	
Which of the above areas need further in-depth observation or assessment?	

SECTION 4. Personal/social development

	Comments
1. Activity level	
Does the child engage in any spontaneous activity?	
Is the child passive most of the time?	

Comments

Is the child constantly active?

Do the child's actions seem to be random or intentional behaviour?

Is the child active in reaction to changes in surroundings?

Is the child's activity directed towards objects, people, or events in the environment?

Does the child withdraw from contact with people or objects?

Is any of the child's activity self-directed? If so, what form does this take?

Does the child engage in stereotyped or bizarre behaviours?

2. Motivation

Does the child need very strong incentives or encouragement to change activity?

What incentives or rewards, eg, food, drink, favourite object, praise, physical contact, are effective with the child?

3. Independence skills

How dependent is the child for satisfaction of personal needs?

Does the child tolerate, cooperate, or actively participate in personal care of self?

How much can the child do unaided in eating and drinking?

How much can the child do unaided in toileting?

How much can the child do unaided in dressing?

How much can the child do unaided in washing?

Comments

Does the child show awareness of own needs, eg, hunger, thirst, discomfort, toileting, attention?

Does the child show any preference for specific people, certain foods or drinks, particular toys or objects, or activities?

Has the child any means of attracting attention?

Has the child any means of indicating needs or preferences?

Is the child capable of taking responsibility for own personal needs?

Is the child willing to take responsibility for own personal needs?

4. Response to demands

Does the child accept and cooperate in activities?

Does the child take an active part in activities?

Does the child withdraw from activities or refuse to take part?

5. Interaction with others

Does the child show awareness of the presence of other people?

Does the child accept physical contact?

Does the child withdraw or resist when approached by others?

Does the child passively accept approaches by others?

Does the child show positive pleasure when approached by others?

Does the child respond to talking directed towards self?

Comments

Does the child respond to talking in general?

Does the child demand attention?

Does the child show different responses with certain people?

Does the child engage in turntaking activities or vocalisations?

Does the child initiate interaction intentionally?

6. Communication

Does the child attend when someone attempts to communicate?

Does the child appear to want to communicate?

Does the child respond appropriately to simple communication through speech?

Does the child respond appropriately to simple communication with gesture, signs, or body cues?

Does the child express need or discomfort by crying, vocalising, or bodily movements?

Does the child communicate consistently through body language or gesture?

Does the child communicate consistently through vocalisation?

Does the child communicate consistently through speech?

Does the child communicate consistently through orthodox signs, eg, *Makaton, Paget-Gorman?*

Does the child communicate consistently through symbols, eg, *Bliss, Rebus, Makaton symbols, Sig-symbols?*

7. Obstructions to learning	Comments
Which are the major barriers to learning in this area?	
8. Detailed assessments	
Which areas require further in-depth observation or assessment?	
Which specialist teachers or other professionals should be involved?	

APPENDIX 2

GENERAL AIMS OF EDUCATION
IN FOUR DEVELOPMENTAL AREAS

Physical development

1. To increase the range and control of self-initiated movements and thereby enable the child to operate effectively within the immediate surroundings.

2. To encourage normal patterns of physical development and prevent abnormal patterns of movement.

3. To improve deformities or dysfunction resulting from the child's disabilities.

4. To encourage confidence in movement and enjoyment of physical activity.

5. To promote perception of movement and postural awareness.

6. To increase self-awareness and enable the child to construct a realistic body image and sense of personal space.

7. To encourage spontaneous movement and ability to control and shape own movements.

8. To improve mobility and locomotor skills.

9. To improve manipulative skills and range and differentiation of fine movements.

Perceptual development

1. To develop perceptual abilities to the fullest possible extent to enable the child to derive and use the maximum amount of information from the surroundings.

2. To encourage the child's awareness of self in relation to the environment and to establish consistent response to change in that environment.

3. To encourage the child to direct attention towards, and concentrate on, the source of stimulation.

4. To promote selective attention to facilitate the development of discrimination in all senses.

5. To increase the acuity of each of the senses to improve the child's ability to discriminate between stimuli in the same modality.

6. To encourage awareness of the different properties of various stimuli to enable the child to form concepts related to sound, vision, touch, taste, smell, and movement.

7. To promote integration of the sensory information which will form the basis of the child's understanding of the surroundings.

Intellectual development

1. To provide experiences and encourage development of cognitive processes which will promote understanding of the immediate surroundings and the society in which the child lives.

2. To promote progress through the early patterns of response to establish intentional and purposeful behaviours.

3. To promote the use of effective learning strategies and a repertoire of actions that will enable the child to exert some degree of control over personal experiences.

4. To promote selection and integration of sensory information and the formation of concepts.

5. To establish interaction with others and ability to maintain mutual attention on external stimuli or referents.

6. To establish a systematic means of communication using the skills which are available to the child.

7. To extend competence in a variety of tasks so that the child can occupy himself appropriately without intervention.

8. To facilitate understanding of familiar surroundings and situations.

9. To establish the ability to make considered choices and appropriate decisions in a variety of situations.

Personal and social development

1. To help the child to develop a positive self-concept and the skills and confidence to become a participating member of society.

2. To encourage the development of qualities and behaviours which will make the child an acceptable member of society.

3. To help the development of tolerance, cooperation, and participation in activities to the maximum extent compatible with the limitations of the child's disability.

4. To encourage awareness of own personal needs and preferences and the ability to make decisions concerning these.

5. To achieve the maximum possible personal independence in eating, drinking, washing, grooming, dressing, and toileting needs.

6. To enable the child to make appropriate decisions and to exert some degree of influence and control over the everyday environment.

7. To encourage awareness of and positive interaction with others.

8. To encourage the development of social skills which will enable the child to be an active member of a group and take part in activities involving sharing, turn-taking, and cooperation with others.

9. To establish a channel of communication which will enable expression of the child's own personality and active participation in social situations.

APPENDIX 3

ASSESSMENTS AND CHECKLISTS

Anson House Preschool Project Papers (Series). Manchester: Univ. of Manchester — Hester Adrian Research Centre, 1982 onwards.

Coupe, J., Barton, L., Barber, M., Collins, L., Levy, D., Murphy, D. *Affective Communication Assessment*. Manchester: Manchester Education Authority, 1985.

Coupe, J., Levy, D. The object related scheme assessment procedure. *Ment. Hand., 1985;* **13**: 1, 22-24.

Dale, F. J. *Progress Guide for Deaf/Blind and/or Severely Handicapped Children. (2nd edn.)*. London: National Deaf/Blind and Rubella Assoc., 1977.

Gerard, K. A. *Checklist of Communicative Competence — 0-2 years, 1985*. (Unpubl.). Avail from: K. A. Gerard, World's End Health Centre, 519-529 King's Road, London, SW10 0UD.

Gunzburg, H. C. *Progress Assessment Chart of Social and Personal Development*. Stratford-on-Avon: SEFA Publications, 1963.

Hebden, H., Whyte, R. A. *Developmental Progress Charts*. Avail. from: Schools' Psychological Service, Blackburn.

Jeffree, D., McConkey, R. *PIP Developmental Charts*. London: Hodder and Stoughton, 1980.

Kiernan, C., Jones, M. C. *Behaviour Assessment Battery*. Windsor: NFER/Nelson, 1982.

Kiernan, C., Reid, B. *Pre-verbal Communication Schedule*. Windsor: NFER/Nelson, 1986.

Locke, A. *Living Language*. Windsor: NFER/Nelson, 1985.

Popovich , D. *A Prescriptive Behavioral Checklist for the Severely and Profoundly Retarded*. Baltimore: Univ. Park Press, 1977.

Presland, J. L. *Paths to Mobility Checklist*. Kidderminster: BIMH Publications, 1982.

Simon, G. B. *The Next Step on the Ladder Development Assessment Scale*. Kidderminster: BIMH Publications, 1986.

Stillman, R. *The Callier-Azusa Scale*. Dallas, Texas: Callier Center for Communication Disorders, 1986.

Uzgiris, I. C., Hunt, J. McV. *Assessment in Infancy: ordinal scales of psychological development*. Urbana Ill.: Univ. Illinois, 1975.

Warner, J. *Helping your Handicapped Child with Early Feeding*. Winslow: Winslow Press, 1981.

APPENDIX 4

SUGGESTED SOURCES
OF IDEAS AND INFORMATION

Audio-visual aids:

Video cassettes

A Sense of Movement, V. Sherborne. Concord Films Council Ltd., 201 Felixstowe Road, Ipswich, Suffolk IP3 9BJ (0473) 726012.

Aspects of Deaf-Blindness, J. F. Dale. Inner London Education Authority Centre for Learning Resources, 275 Kennington Lane, London, SE11 5QZ (01-633) 5974.

Curriculum Development through Observation — The Multisensory Approach. Wren Spinney School, Westover Road, Kettering, Northants. NN16 0AP (0536) 81939.

In Touch, V. Sherborne. Concord Films Council Ltd.

Making Progress, P. Caldwell. Concord Films Council Ltd.

The Needs of the Profoundly Handicapped. Jordanhill College of Education, 76 Southbrae Drive, Glasgow, G13 1PP (041-959) 1232.

Audio cassettes

Body Awareness, Contact, Communication, C. and M. Knill. LDA/Living and Learning, Duke Street, Wisbech, Cambs. PE13 2AE (0945) 63441.

Fun Fair: a Drama Games Event. Inner London Education Authority Consortium, Resources for Learning Difficulties. Jack Tizard School, Finlay Street, London SW6 6HB (01-736) 8877.

Tape slide set

Galaxies: a Multisensory Experience. ILEA Consortium

Equipment to make:

Caston, D. *Easy-to-make Toys for Your Handicapped Child.* London: Souvenir Press, 1983.

Lear, R. *Play Helps: Toys and Activities for Handicapped Children.* London: Heinemann, 1977.

Mitchell, S., Ouvry, C. *Make it Simple: Easy-to-make Toys for Profoundly Handicapped Children.* 1985 (unpubl.). Avail from: S. Mitchell, Poplar Grange Cottage, 33, Cross Lane, Crookes, Sheffield 10, or C. Ouvry, 2, Rotherwood Road, London SW15.

Riddick, B. *Toys and Play for the Handicapped Child.* London: Croom Helm, 1982.

Play Matters (National Toy Libraries Association and ACTIVE). *Active Worksheets.* Avail from: 68 Churchway, London NW1 1LT (01-387 9592).

Equipment to buy:

A-2-B Toys for the Disabled - Castle Donnington Community College, Mount Pleasant, Castle Donnington, Derby DE7 2LN (0332) 812401.

Bradford Activity Toys — 103 Dockfield Road, Shipley, West Yorkshire, BD17 7AR (0274) 596030.

Consortium — Resources for Learning Difficulties, Jack Tizard School, Finlay Street, London SW6 6HB (01-736) 8877.

Edu-play — 10 Vestry Street, Leicester LE1 1WQ (0533) 25827.

Huntercraft — Ramsam Stable, Priestlands Lane, Sherborne, Dorset DT9 4PD (0935) 812288.

Joncare — 7 Ashville Trading Estate, Nuffield Way, Abingdon, Oxon. (0235) 28120/29353.

Mangar Aids Ltd. — Units 1 & 2, Presteigne Industrial Estate, Presteigne, Powys (0544) 267674.

NACRO Handicap Aids Workshop — Unit 9 Sandy Way, Amington Industrial Estate, Tamworth, Staffs. B77 4DS (0827) 51587.

Ortho-Kinetics (UK) Ltd. — 190 Commerical Road, Totton, Southampton SO4 3ZZ (0703) 863629.

Quest Educational Designs Ltd. — 1 Prince Alfred Street, Gosport, Hants. PO12 1QH (0705) 581179.

Rompa-Pressure Sealed Plastics Ltd. — PO Box 5, Wheatbridge Road, Chesterfield, Derbyshire S40 2AE (0246) 211777.

Toys for the Handicapped — 76 Barracks Road, Sandy Lane Industrial Estate, Stourport-on-Severn, Worcs. DY13 9QB (02993) 78820.

Vibro-Medico — 20 Church Road, Hadleigh, Essex SS7 2DQ (0702) 557966.

Periodicals:

Information Exchange RNIB, 224 Great Portland Street, London W1N 6AA.

Mental Handicap BIMH Publications, Foley Industrial Park, Stourport Road, Kidderminster, Worcs. DY11 7QG.

Special Children — 73, All Saints Road, Kings Heath, Birmingham, B14 7LN.

Special Education — National Council for Special Education, 1 Wood Street, Stratford-upon-Avon, Warwickshire, CV37 6JE.

Talking Sense — SENSE-National Deaf-Blind and Rubella Association, 311 Gray's Inn Road, London WC1X 8PT.

Index